DOXOLOGY in DARKNESS

A family who loved through tragedy

ISBN: 978-1-947319-37-0

Cover and text layout design: Kristi Yoder

Printed in the USA

Published by:

TGS International
P.O. Box 355
Berlin, Ohio 44610 USA
Phone: 330.893.4828
Fax: 330.893.2305
www.tgsinternational.com

TGS001641

DOXOLOGY in DARKNESS

A family who loved through tragedy

Rachael Lofgren

To be grateful for an unanswered prayer,
to give thanks in an interior sense of desolation,
to trust in the love of God in the face of the
marvels, cruel circumstances, obscenities,
and common places of life is to whisper
a doxology in darkness.

–Brennan Manning

Table of Contents

Dedication

To G.J. Hoffman:

No David could ask for a better Jonathan. I treasure you
and the friendship and memories we share. Most of all I
treasure our shared bond in Christ. Whatever the cost, He's
worth it all! May He receive the reward of His sufferings in
our lives and in our friendship. I love you, always!

Afraid? Of What?

To feel the spirit's glad release?
To pass from pain to perfect peace,
The strife and strain of life to cease?
Afraid—of that?
Afraid? Of what?

Afraid to see the Savior's face
To hear His welcome and to trace
The glory gleam from wounds of grace?
Afraid—of that?
Afraid? Of what?

A flash, a crash, a pierced heart;
Darkness, light, oh, heaven's art!
A wound of His a counterpart!
Afraid—of that?
Afraid? Of what?

To do by death what life could not—
Baptize with blood a stony plot,
Till souls shall blossom from the spot?
Afraid—of that?[1]

—E. H. Hamilton

---

[1] Hamilton, E H. Afraid? Of What?: And Other Poems and Sketches. Bristol, TN: E.H. Hamilton and King College, 1970.

1

Feed Sack Church House

T he gears of the blue SUV ground into low as the vehicle slid through the mud. Another turn in the mountain road, and a little coffee shack came into view, perched high on a mountain beside a rushing stream. Heavy tropical rain ran in rivulets along the windshield as the Kropf family pulled up outside the shack where they met for church that fall of 1996. *We'll hardly be able to hear ourselves sing today,* twenty-year-old Rebecca Kropf surmised as she glanced at the heavy clouds overhead.

> O gracious God, thy pleasure
> Is in thy Christ made known,
> And tells the boundless measure
> Of blessing for thine own . . .[1]

The words of the hymn, sung in Spanish, were indeed nearly drowned out by the happy drumming of rain on the tin roof. Rebecca glanced

---

[1] Cenita Thompson (1822–1909).

at the faces around her and sang alto with all her heart. The sonorous voice of her younger brother Michael held the deep notes with her father Dennis's tenor. Minister Luis Suarez's hearty bass kept time. The clear voices of her younger sisters, Rosy and Esther, carried melody while all the others mingled their various parts in joyful praise. Even though clouds blotted out the sun that morning, Rebecca found it easy to lift her heart in praise in this setting, surrounded by her family and other believers. No one in the little group would have guessed the trials ahead that would test their commitment to worship God through all of life.

It was another Sunday morning at the new outreach church in Agua Caliente, Costa Rica. The Kropf family and the Suarez family, both from the Christian Mennonite Fellowship in San Vito, traveled the two-and-a-half hours one way over gravel roads every Sunday to hold services in this remote area. These two families had been chosen from their community to begin a sister church. Since Luis was a minister, the church in San Vito had asked him to lead out in the endeavor. Within a few months, the Kropfs and the Suarezes were planning to move to Agua Caliente.

Sometimes in the gray predawn of a Sunday morning as Rebecca stumbled about getting ready for church, she wondered if it was worth all the effort. But the smiles on the faces as they sang the Spanish hymns always assured her that it was. At times in those first months, up to thirty local people would gather with them to worship in Spanish. Tucked among these hidden hills, people waited, hungering for truth. *Surely no distance is too great to travel to reach them!* Rebecca thought. Her heart warmed as she saw the eager attention some of the newcomers gave Brother Luis as he read the text of his sermon.

She looked around the interior of the vacant coffee shack where they were meeting. For the present, they held services wherever they could find space and a roof over their heads. How nice it would be once they had their own permanent church building and were settled on their own farm!

On the drive home after church, the two families stopped by a river to eat lunch. The rain had cleared a bit, and the sun peered languidly down on them. When the men had parked the vehicles, the young people quickly helped carry the lunch provisions to a sunny spot of grass.

"Let's eat down near the water," Rebecca suggested to the rest of the girls. After grace was said, all the girls took their sandwiches and picked their way over the tumbled rocks that lined the steep riverbank.

"Here, let me make sure there aren't any snakes hanging out here." Esther, always assertive and determined to do things right, energetically beat at the stones and the long grass to frighten away any of the 162 species of snakes that inhabit Costa Rica.[2] High in the branches of a giant *guanacaste*[3] tree a slight breezed danced, sending a few leathery brown elephant-ear-shaped seed pods rattling to the ground. The piercing song of a golden-winged warbler sounded from a shrub nearby.

"Isn't this lovely?" Fourteen-year-old Leah Grace Suarez situated herself on a smooth rock. "What kind of sandwiches did your family bring today?"

"Meat salad." Esther munched her first bite hungrily. "Why, what kind did you bring?"

"Bologna." Leah Grace sounded less than enthused. "I think your family and ours should make lunch for each other sometime and see what happens. Wouldn't that be fun?"

"It could be fun for something different," Esther said. Leah Grace caught the sparkle of fun in Esther's eyes. "Girls, we just about need an adventure on an afternoon like this, don't you think?"

Rebecca yawned. "I'm ready for a nap. Or a good long talk."

"I guess you must be getting old." Rosy elbowed Rebecca teasingly.

"Last time I checked, Sunday was a day of rest," Rebecca returned

---

[2] "The Reptiles of Costa Rica," Imagenes Tropicales, San José, Costa Rica, 2014, <http://www.travelcostarica.nu/reptiles>, accessed on April 26, 2017.

[3] Pronounced *gooah nah CAHS teh*

saucily, her brown eyes warm with good humor.

The conversation drifted to more serious matters as the girls discussed the sermon and its personal applications. "I've been thinking about baptism recently," Leah Grace said. "I still recall your baptism day so clearly, Esther. Remember when I would come sit in on your instruction class?"

"Yes, it was a pretty big class of applicants. There were seven of us to start out with. Then only three of us were baptized that Sunday."

"And remember, María José was there with her new baby boy, Amidio?" Rebecca said. "He was so, so cute."

"And tiny too!" Esther said. "We girls all gathered around him and took turns oohing and ahhing over him."

"You were nervous that day, weren't you?" Rebecca asked with her typical analytical perception.

"Yes, a little bit. But Brother Richard told us exactly what we would be expected to say, and it was easier than I thought it would be. Saying baptismal vows is a sobering thing, but it's easy to forget to carry that seriousness into every day of life. I truly want to be faithful."

Rosy gazed contemplatively at the swiftly moving water of the river below them. Her green-gray eyes reflected the sunlight that danced on its moving surface, her face a study of unspoken thoughts. *I've yielded my life to Jesus too. I think I would be ready to take the step of baptism in the next year or two.*

· ·

The Kropf family was the first to move. In February of 1997 their old Toyota SUV puttered up the last long rise of Pittier Mountain to the little pink tin-roofed rancho they had rented. Along the one-kilometer stretch of road that ascended from the village to the Kropfs' new home, curious neighbors had paused from their work and responded to the friendly greeting eighteen-year-old Michael had yelled out from his position on the back of the vehicle. He loved this local custom—a friendly exchange between those in vehicles and those on foot.

Perched atop the mountain, the house offered a splendid view. The family was in the process of purchasing a large farm, but until they had buildings and a corral, they would rent temporary facilities from a nearby farmer for their ten-cow dairy operation.

"What will it be like living without electricity?" Rebecca wondered aloud to Esther as the two sisters unpacked dishes and arranged them on the kitchen shelves.

"It'll be different, for sure. And no phone, either, unless we go into town." Esther sighed apprehensively.

Rebecca wrote home to their community in San Vito about it all later. "This new situation is rough and lonely sometimes. I don't think I'll ever complain about being too busy again. We just LIVE for the Sundays, when people come for church." She sealed the letter with an ache in her heart. Growing up in Central America was the only life she had known; she could scarcely remember when, at the age of three, she had moved with her family from Pulaski, Tennessee, to Costa Rica. Already she longed for the comfortable familiarity of their home in San Vito.

"But Lord, you are worth it to me," she prayed as she knelt by her bed that night. "And souls getting saved are worth it to me. Help us to do your will, joyfully and without complaint. You gave everything. I want to give you everything."

Some months later Luis and Esther Suarez moved with their six lively youngsters to a little coffee shack they fixed up, situated across the hollow from where the Kropfs were building a shop. When the Kropfs moved into the shop to live, a path was soon worn between the two houses. Later the boys built a lovely little bridge across the creek that ran through the bottom of the hollow.

Sometimes when they weren't busy with farm chores and making cheese, the girls would run barefoot through the verdant jungle shrubbery, down the steep slope to the bridge. There they would sit with their feet dangling over the edge, soaking in the warm beauty of their surroundings.

One day Luis and Esther's littlest child Evelyn wandered off. When they couldn't find her, they raised the alarm, and the Kropfs joined in the search. They found the two-year-old on the bridge, watching the water and exclaiming as it bubbled over the rocks. Evelyn was the only little one in the church, and everyone adored her. Her Down syndrome features and ways made her extra lovable and vulnerable. Right after the incident, the boys built a gate on the Suarez's side of the bridge to protect the little girl from falling into the water if she were ever to find her way down to the bridge alone again.

The farm the Kropfs were purchasing was the most envied farm in the area. Its ridged, mountainous hills plunged into burbling creeks at the bottom of every hollow. Lush pasture and tropical forest rolled over the acreage in a varied landscape. The black, loamy soil was feet deep and promised to yield a bountiful harvest. But it was wild and uncultivated, and the family poured hours and hours of backbreaking labor into taming it into a homestead.

Even simple daily tasks like washing clothes, milking, and making cheese were all done by hand. Since the Suarez family owned twenty cows and the Kropf family owned ten, all that milking built strong hands in their young people. Sometimes it built strong backs too. Or at least sore ones.

"Daddy and Luis are both gone tonight," Michael told Esther and Leah Grace as the young people traipsed up the road toward the corral for evening milking. Ever since Kenneth, the Kropf firstborn, had gotten married, Michael took more responsibility for the farm work. "I guess we'll have to haul the milk back by hand or something. Think we're strong enough, David?" The eighteen-year-old slapped his younger friend on the shoulder and grinned. The blue Toyota that they normally used to haul the milk was not available this time.

"Oh, I think so," David Suarez agreed stoutly. At thirteen he hated to admit defeat in anything. Later that night Esther would recount to Rebecca and Rosy what followed.

"We worked quickly, moving from cow to cow and filling the corral with our usual banter and singing while we milked. When we finished milking, two tall, ten-gallon cans and two five-gallon buckets of milk stood waiting outside the corral gate for us to haul."

Rebecca listened eagerly to the details. If there was anything she loved, it was a good family story.

"Leah Grace and I exchanged glances, and Leah Grace smiled bravely, but her eyes looked doubtful as she eyed those milk cans. I knew she was wondering if we could do it." Esther chuckled. "I was kind of wondering myself."

"That does sound like a load!" Rebecca said sympathetically.

"Michael spoke right up, as he usually does, 'If you girls think you can take the taller can, David and I will take the other can and the two buckets. Do you think you can do it?'

"We girls promised to try. But before we had our cans in position between us, the boys had grabbed the other can between them and each had taken a bucket in his free hand. 'Okay, heave ho, and off we go,' I heard Michael say as he took off with his steady stride. 'Only half a kilometer to home! Goodbye, cows—and goodbye, girls.' He winked at me, and we started off."

Rebecca's eyes crinkled in a merry grin, and Rosy chuckled. "I can just imagine the scene," Rebecca laughed. "You and Leah Grace huffing and puffing along. One of you taller than the other with that big old can between you!"

"And was it ever heavy!" Esther shook her head slowly as if she still couldn't believe they had made it. "The milk sloshed against the sides of the can, and both of us breathed heavily after the first quarter of the way. Already the boys had far outpaced us.

" 'Wait for us!' I called after them.

" 'What's taking you so long?' Michael asked. But I knew he was just teasing. The boys set their buckets down and flopped on the grass to rest till we girls caught up.

" 'I can't do this anymore. My arm feels like it's falling off,' Leah Grace told me at this point." Esther stood up and dramatized her friend.

"I can so see it!" Rebecca's eyes twinkled.

"I tried valiantly to shift the load to make it easier on her. 'It's hard,' I told her, 'but we're going to make it, Leah Grace. I know it. We aren't quitters, and we won't quit, will we?'

" 'We can't,' she said. 'But my shoulder aches like fire. Do you really think we can make it all the way home?'

"I told her I thought we could do it if we kept helping each other. My arms felt ready to fall off too, but I thought we could do it."

"Poor girl," Rosy said.

"As the road dragged on, we felt the strain more and more. When we finally dragged the can into the yard, we let go of those handles with a big sigh of relief and fell into each other's arms for a victory hug. 'See, we did it!' we cheered. And I will probably dream of lugging cans in my sleep tonight," Esther finished.

After housing for their families, the church house was next on the building agenda. Together the Kropf and Suarez men built a pole building with a tin roof. The women and girls washed an astounding number of feed sacks by hand, and after they had dried in the sun, they set to work sewing them into "walls."

"We'll have our own feed sack church house when we're finished."

Esther straightened her back from bending over her sewing. "Perhaps it will look a little like the tabernacle in the Old Testament."

"Except it won't be movable," Rebecca added with a laugh.

"It will be good to have a church house of our own." Judy, the girls' mother, surveyed their work with a smile. Eventually they would have to replace the walls because of the dampness and mold. But when the sacks were all hung in their proper places, the little group shared the joy and satisfaction of an ingenious job well done.

2

In the Coffee Patch

Rain fell incessantly. Hurricane Mitch could be thanked for that. Honduras and Nicaragua felt the worst of the storm, the second deadliest Atlantic hurricane on record. But Costa Rica received her share of its tears that late autumn of 1998.

Rebecca brushed aside a dripping coffee branch and tossed another glossy red berry into her basket. "Hey, Esther, how's your rain slicker holding out?" she called across the row.

"Oh, all right, I think. I'm partly dry anyway." Esther's grin showed that the drizzle hadn't dampened her indomitable spirit. She adjusted the plastic trash bag she was wearing. With three slits—one for her head and one for each arm—the bags made cheap disposable rain gear for the long, wet days in the coffee patch. "I think that idea of keeping our hair and veils dry with smaller plastic bags might have been the best one we've come up with this year," she added. "It makes you feel the dampness less if your head isn't soaking."

"I agree!" Leah Grace piped up from the opposite row. "I don't think we've ever seen this much rain in one coffee harvest!"

The Kropf young people and several of the Suarez youth earned some extra cash by working on the coffee plantations in Agua Caliente.

"Someone said that thousands have died due to the flooding from this hurricane." Michael picked carefully, searching out the ripest berries. "They estimate that over a million are homeless. No doubt those numbers will be higher before the storm's damages are over."

"Those poor people," Rosy said. "We ought to pray for them."

"We certainly can't complain about a little rain!" Rebecca swung the basket attached to her waist to one side and trudged through the mud to the end of her row. Pouring the bright red coffee berries into a burlap sack, she went back with her empty basket to where she had left off picking. "I think sometimes it's easy for me to be less than grateful. I take too many things for granted."

"I know what you mean," Esther said.

"Since we moved out here to Agua Caliente last year, I've realized that more than ever," Rebecca said. "Sometimes I miss having electricity and being close to our larger community of family and friends. Then I have to remind myself that every soul being reached here with the Gospel is so much more important than my own comfort. It's a privilege to give our lives to the Lord in this way; it's just easy to forget when we wish for something else sometimes."

"Eeek!" Esther slid on a muddy incline and grabbed at a coffee shrub for support. "It's slick over here!"

"Are you drowning?" Michael's eyes twinkled. "Need a team effort over there?"

"Oh, you!" Esther laughed. "I'm not an ox, you know."

"It's still hard for me to imagine that oxen really used to drown in those mudholes Daddy talks about," Rebecca said.

"Oxen actually drowned?" Leah Grace's eyes widened.

"Legend has it." Michael went to empty his brimming basket, squishing through the thick mud. "They say teams would get so mired down with their loads of coffee berries that they would thrash around in a mudhole till they died. The farmers started going to town in groups so they could use more than one team at a time to pull the carts through."

"That must have been some really deep mud!" Leah Grace exclaimed.

The morning wore on, and soon it was time to stop for lunch. Standing around in their dripping black trash bags, the hungry workers devoured coffee and sandwiches and went back to work with a will. "Just a couple more hours till four o'clock, and we'll be finished for the day," they encouraged each other.

On a good day each picker averaged around a hundred pounds of coffee berries. After processing, it amounted to about twenty pounds of ready-to-grind coffee beans.

After an afternoon of steady drizzle, at last it was time to quit. Rebecca and Rosy took their baskets over to the coffee shack at the edge of the patch. Michael and Leah Grace's two younger brothers carried their loads of hundred-pound sacks over their shoulders. With just a few baskets and a partly filled sack of coffee left, Esther and Leah Grace agreed to carry it between them, which proved difficult.

Slipping in the mud, Leah Grace regained her balance and tried to compensate for the unwieldy baskets she balanced on her hip and the bulky sack she carried by one corner. With the opposite corner of the sack tucked firmly in her fists, Esther pulled backward and staggered a little at the momentum. "Ooh, I feel like I'm skating in muck!" she squealed.

"Careful!" Leah Grace laughed. "We'll both fall in the mud, and then think what a sight we'll be for all to behold."

The rain began falling in earnest again, and it dribbled down their faces and dripped in their eyes. They tried to avoid the soupy spots, lugging their wet sack and breathing hard from exertion. Dodging dripping coffee branches that caught at them as they ducked past, they squealed breathlessly when they slipped on an especially slimy spot.

Suddenly the pair lurched to a stop. Leah Grace's boot stuck deep in the mud, and her stocking foot lurched out and plunged into the mud ahead of her. "Eww!" she wailed in surprise.

Taking a look at her friend with one boot and one sock mired in mud, Esther burst into peals of laughter.

"I feel like crying." Leah Grace looked at her foot in disgust. "How am I supposed to walk all the way back to the shack with no boot?" She pulled her foot out of the muck and leaned back to reach the stray boot, but it was too far away for her to balance the sack and rescue her boot.

"Find a place to put the sack down, and see if you can get it out," she suggested to Esther.

Wiping rain and tears of laughter from her eyes with the back of her hand, Esther took the full weight of the sack and set it under a coffee plant. Coming back, she reached for the boot and gave it a hard tug. It gave a sucking sound but hardly budged, and it took several more hard yanks before she was finally able to free it. "Here you go." She tossed the boot to Leah Grace and wiped her muddy hands gingerly on her wet rain slicker to clean them.

Leah Grace tugged off her muddy sock and stuck her foot carefully in the rescued boot. "Now what am I supposed to do with this?" She held the long, muddy sock toward Esther imploringly. "I don't want to put it in my pocket, and both of my hands are full with the coffee sack."

Esther lugged the sack back out from under the dripping coffee plant and rejoined her friend. "Here, stick it in on top of the coffee."

Struggling and sliding, they made the rest of the trip to the shack without major incident. When they arrived, everyone was already sitting around, and the boss had begun to measure coffee in the *cajuela*,[1] a square tin container about the size of a bushel. The Indian harvesters

---

[1] Pronounced *kah HOOEH lah*

were laughing among themselves, waiting to see who had harvested the largest quantity that day. It was always a competition.

When Esther and Leah Grace joined the group, Michael saw them and came over. "What took you so long?" he asked.

Glancing around at the people milling about them, Esther lowered her voice. "Oh, the mud just delayed us a bit." Her eyes twinkled. Taking their partly filled sack from them, Michael went back to helping the boss pour out the beans for measurement.

Weary from the day's work and relieved to be finished, Esther and Leah Grace sat down to rest. They watched as the red berries tumbled merrily from the sacks. How delightful to simply be under a roof and out of the rain for a little while! Suddenly their rest was interrupted as the Tico[2] boss reached into one of the sacks and held up a long dirty stocking. *"¿De quién es este calcetín?"*[3] With a laugh, he asked whose sock it was.

Leah Grace turned startled eyes to Esther's face. "We forgot the sock!" she gasped in horror.

Rebecca and Rosy looked on in puzzled amusement.

The boss still dangled the sock high, his dark eyes twinkling with humor as he surveyed the group of harvesters. There was no escaping it. Blushing with embarrassment, Leah Grace claimed her possession.

"I'm sorry we forgot," Esther apologized to her anguished friend.

"Don't worry," Leah Grace smiled. "It could have happened to anyone with all this mud."

"It really could have," Rebecca added her comfort as they headed home. "Don't feel badly, Leah Grace. It was funny, though! I could hardly keep from laughing! It didn't cast a bad light on you. It was just really comical!"

"I don't know why they didn't want a sock in their coffee," Michael teased. "It would have added a lot of flavor."

---

[2] Costa Rican

[3] Pronounced *deh kee EHN ehs EH seh kahl seh TEEN*

3

"Isn't It Beautiful?"

Dawn crept in through a thick curtain of fog that July morning in San Vito, where the Kropf family had returned to make their home. During their two years in Agua Caliente, the congregation had slowly dwindled. Finally the church had dissolved, and in 1999, the families who had initiated the sister church moved back to San Vito. One bright spot in the midst of the disappointments had been the conversion of Estella. Despite her husband's strong opposition to her baptism, she went ahead in obedience to her newfound Savior. She spoke her baptismal vows loud and clear, and the radiance on her face as she confessed Christ publicly filled the little congregation with holy joy.

That morning as she had her devotions, Rebecca thought of Estella and thanked God for helping that little woman remain faithful. Those years in a remote setting without electricity or a phone had not been easy. But God had granted some fruit. Even one soul was worth it all!

The fog vanished as the first rays of sunlight shone over the mountains across the valley. Only wisps of clouds were left to blanket the mountain formation, which the locals referred to as the "Sleeping Indian." As Rebecca rose from her knees and gazed out the window, she thought, *Perhaps someday the fog will vanish and we'll see more clearly God's purposes in the things He allows.*

"*¡Upe! ¡Upe!*"[1] A man's voice called from outside the house, jarring Rebecca out of her reverie. She went to the door to find her brother Kenneth announcing his arrival in typical Costa Rican fashion. Eighteen-month-old Victor, in Kenneth's arms, reached out for Rebecca.

Rebecca, Rosy, and Esther exchanged knowing smiles as they received their nephew with open arms.

"He's yours for the day." Kenneth, married to Geraldina, was the only married sibling in the Kropf family so far. Victor was the much-loved only nephew of the clan, but before the day was over, he would be joined by a sibling.

When Kenneth had gone, Rosy looked at Rebecca sympathetically. "Too bad you have to go to school today."

"Well, you all better tell me as soon as the news comes, regardless of whether I'm teaching school or not," Rebecca spoke emphatically.

Esther hugged little Victor to her and stroked his soft brown hair. "I wonder if it will be a brother or a sister." Her blue eyes twinkled in anticipation. "I can't wait to have another nephew or niece to spoil."

When Rebecca had trudged off up the hill to the schoolhouse and the morning work had been done, Esther and Rosy decided it was the perfect morning to take their nephew for a walk outdoors. Singing and laughing, they headed for the creek.

Meanwhile Rebecca busied herself in her classroom, getting ready for her students to arrive. "I love teaching," she thought aloud, glancing out the window as the first students came in the lane. "But on days like today it takes a little extra faithfulness, I guess." She could picture her sisters

---

[1] Pronounced *OO pay*

heading to the ravine with her nephew even now. Pushing aside a brief pang of envy, Rebecca focused on her students with a smile.

After half-sliding, half-climbing down the steep bank of the ravine, Esther and Rosy shed their boots and splashed into the burbling stream. "Isn't it lovely?" Esther threw back her head to take in the deep blue of the sky. Her eyes swept the green banks rising above them and the creek tumbling and singing away below them. "And God saw all that He had made, and behold, it was very good," she quoted joyfully.

" 'Ood, 'ood," Victor copied his aunt. His brown eyes sparkled with pleasure.

"Let's climb higher and see what's around the next bend," Rosy suggested. *See what's around the next bend.* Were those words echoing across the ravine, or was it Rosy's imagination? Truly, God was merciful in sheltering these two women from knowledge of the ghastly scene that would take place in another ravine nearby.

But that darkness still belonged to the unknown years ahead. Basking in the sunshine, Esther climbed over yet another fallen log and exclaimed, "Here's a waterfall!"

"Here, take Victor. I want to see too." Rosy passed him to Esther's waiting arms and clambered over the log, her wet skirt sloshing after her. Peering over the edge of the drop-off in the stream, she exclaimed, "We've got to get down there some way. It looks so nice and inviting!"

"We'll have to go around and come in from the other side of the waterfall to get there," Esther analyzed quickly. Clambering up the edge of the ravine, they circled around to the other side and, undaunted by the steepness of the grade, slid down an even steeper bank to the delightful pool.

"Oh! It's lovely!" Esther squealed. The waterfall was a merry cascade no more than seven feet from top to bottom. It sprayed a fine mist into the air as it flowed ceaselessly into the mirror-like pool that spread in buoyant, bubbling ripples at its base.

Victor plunged both chubby fists into the clear, cool water and slurped from them thirstily. Then churning his legs, he squealed with rapture. "Look at him!" Rosy giggled. Esther chuckled, and Victor laughed out loud.

Esther splashed Rosy, and Rosy squealed. "Watch out!" she warned, laughing. Esther spluttered and laughed, ducking away too late from a spray of water Rosy aimed skillfully at her face.

After a few minutes they stopped to catch their breath before heading back to the house to make dinner. "When have we had so much fun?" Rosy wondered.

"It's a day to celebrate," Esther laughed. She hugged Victor to her and kissed the top of his head. "It reminds me a little bit of the day we were waiting for this kind of news the first time."

"But somehow it feels different now that we know how fun it is to have a nephew. Like even more special or something," Rosy mused.

Pausing during a quiet moment at school, Rebecca, too, was remembering the day their first nephew was born. Her eyes grew hazy with the memories, both sweet and sad at once. In the midst of their delight at the safe birth of Kenneth and Geraldina's baby, sadness had pierced their hearts when they found out the baby was to be named Victor Leonard.

Leonard had been their second oldest brother. Physically strong and steady in character, he had been an unusually deep thinker and a hard worker before a farm accident fourteen years earlier claimed his life at only eleven years old. It had been the first major tragedy the family faced in Costa Rica, and it had left its mark on all of them. But his mother had taken it the hardest.

The morning of January 8, 1985, had started as usual with the family conversing around the breakfast table.

"We found a dead chick in the henhouse this morning," Kenneth reported.

"Well, a dead chick in the barn is better than a dead chick in the house." With the protective pride of a mother hen, Judy smiled at her "chicks" seated around the table.

"Can we have bread for breakfast?" Leonard, who loved bread, asked his mother.

Judy had smiled and pointed to the empty cupboard behind him, then gestured toward the loaves of bread rising on the counter. "There will be bread for dinner," she had promised.

It was the dry season of a drought year, and the ground had cracked open with thirst. They had to monitor the water they pumped from the well. Dennis had sent Leonard to do this job, since he had plans to make a repair that day and needed the water pumped down to a certain level. When Leonard removed the tin cover from the well, the wire that brought electricity to the pump caught on a jagged edge of tin that sliced through the insulation, sending an aggressive current of power through the metal and into his body.

Judy heard his cries from the house. "Run and help him, Rebecca!" she cried. Rebecca raced down into the gully to help her older brother. She saw him kneeling by the well, but by the time she reached him, he was slumped over as if he were falling in. Thinking that he needed to be pulled out, she grabbed him, only to feel a shock go through her arm. Alarmed, she jerked back. Later Judy said it was a miracle she didn't die too. Leonard had rubber boots on, but Rebecca was barefoot.

By the time they all reached the scene, his cries had ebbed away. Somehow Dennis got him away from the metal and laid him out on the dry ground. Desperately he worked over his son, trying to restore life through mouth-to-mouth resuscitation. Judy stood tearfully at the top of the bank with her two youngest girls, Esther and Rosy, clinging to her skirt. Finally, when it seemed Leonard would not revive, Judy called down to Dennis brokenly, "If the Lord took him, let's accept that. Let's not try and try to bring him back, Dennis."

Dennis's strong shoulders had slumped in sorrow and his large hands had rested on his son's chest to feel a final time that life had truly fled. Never again would he feel that strong, young heartbeat. Dennis took comfort later in remembering how Leonard had spoken to him the night before the accident about the book of Revelation. His eyes had been thoughtful as he remarked, "Isn't it beautiful, Daddy? It has so many nice things in it. I like to read it." No one had guessed that he would soon be experiencing that heavenly beauty firsthand.

The simple funeral had passed quickly, but the grief had stayed. Rebecca often found her mother weeping in a quiet corner. Kenneth, who was reserved by nature, took his brother's death the hardest of the children. At thirteen, he was old enough to absorb the sorrow. Even though Rebecca and her younger siblings grieved for the duration of a child's grief and then moved on with normal life, the trauma and the miracle of her own life being preserved impacted Rebecca deeply.

Now only memories and a grave marked Leonard's earthly existence. But his family would never forget. That's why it had been both sweet and sad when Kenneth, years after the accident, had chosen to name his first-born son after his brother.

That afternoon as Rebecca checked lessons after school, her mind wandered again and again to her sister-in-law laboring to bring a child into the world. Could something have gone wrong? Had the baby arrived? With a sigh, she picked up her pen to grade yet another paper. How could she focus on her work with such an important event taking place nearby?

Suddenly someone on the road below the church house called her name. Flying to the door, she saw Kenneth standing there with an umbrella in his hand. He was headed down to tell his parents the news. "In a little while you'll want to go see Ezra Joshua!" he called. A huge grin covered his bearded face.

"Ezra! It's a boy!" Rebecca shouted joyfully.

A few minutes later the entire family piled into the Toyota for the short but steep jaunt down the road to Kenneth's house. When Rebecca saw the blue SUV lumbering up and down the hills on the lane leading from the Kropfs' home to the road, she sprinted down the hill from the schoolhouse to join them.

"Now, listen." Kenneth turned to his younger siblings as they pulled up to the little house with its long veranda and weathered board siding. "Don't act like a wild bunch of savages when we get there, okay?"

They filed into the house with properly subdued excitement, and Judy went into the bedroom to congratulate Geraldina and bring the little fellow out for all to see. She came back beaming, her eyes radiant with tender grandmother love. She pulled back the covers at one end of the bundle to reveal a red cherubic face resembling Victor's. Victor seemed somber and thoughtful as he beheld the little man who had suddenly joined their family.

The three *tías*[2] (aunts) were wild with delight, squealing and exclaiming over his darling little toes and long fingers. He was passed from arm to arm as everyone took a turn holding him and hugging him. Even Michael cradled him in his strong *tío*[3] (uncle) arms, enjoying his newest nephew.

Rebecca looked into his little face and marveled at the miracle of birth, kissing his downy head. A fleeting pain stabbed her heart at the thought of some of the children in their neighborhood who were growing up in dysfunctional families. *Every baby deserves to be as loved and celebrated as you are, little Ezra,* she thought.

---

[2] Singular form is pronounced *TEE ah*

[3] Pronounced *TEE oh*

4

"I Have to Call You Daddy"

"I wish a stable family could take Marco[1] in and give him a home." Concern etched Dennis's face as he ate Sunday dinner with the rest of the family. "He looked miserable today in church."

"No one would wonder why with a home life like his." Rebecca spooned *gallo pinto,*[2] rice and beans flavored with Worcestershire sauce, onto her plate and passed the dish to Michael. "I know his Grandma Lola tries, but with his mother's lifestyle, he gets exposed to all sorts of vile things." His grandmother had become part of the Mennonite church in San Vito. Both Marco and José[3] were related to Kenneth's wife Geraldina. José was Marco's uncle, but being nearly the same age made the boys more like cousins. Neither of the two little boys knew a father's love.

"Lola was telling me that as soon as Marco gets to her house, he begs to wear some of José's clothes, and when he leaves with his mother again,

---

[1] Name changed to protect privacy

[2] Pronounced *GAH yoh PEEN toh*

[3] Name changed to protect privacy

he cries and says that he doesn't want to be worldly. I can't imagine what he must suffer sometimes," Rebecca spoke compassionately. "Being the same age and such close friends with his uncle José makes it hard for him to be back and forth so much too. He misses him like a brother, José told me in school one day. And he's pretty far behind in his learning too."

"Hasn't the ministry offered to place him in one of the church family's homes?" Michael inquired between bites of chicken.

"Yes, they have," Dennis said. "Let's continue to pray that God would open the right doors as He wills so Marco can grow up to know Him."

The phone call from their pastor the following day took the family by surprise. None of them had considered that they might be the ones asked to take the nine-year-old boy into their home. They were one of the two church couples who didn't have young children left at home, but Judy's poor health, the fact that they were already in their sixties, and their present economic standing made them hesitant to consider taking on the responsibility of raising another child. For several years Judy had suffered from a heart condition, persistent headaches, and chronic exhaustion. "We'll pray about it," Dennis told the ministry.

"I hesitate to take him," Judy confided to Rebecca in the midst of the decision.

Rebecca looked up from the laundry she was folding and nodded. "Because of Delmar?"

"Yes. We tried so hard with him, but we couldn't help him in the end." Judy blinked back tears.

"I know that was so hard for you, Mama. You did so well and loved so hard, but it makes it difficult to risk again, doesn't it?" Rebecca's brown eyes reflected tender concern. She knew how sensitive her mom was. Judy's heart had been crushed by the waywardness of an adopted son eighteen years before, and she didn't want to face the pain all over again.

The boy had been abandoned, and the welfare department had asked the Kropf family if they would take him in. They had agreed and had begun the process of adoption for the small, dark-eyed boy they named Delmar. He was Esther's age, and since all their other children were still school age at the time, it seemed ideal that Delmar would grow up with the other children in the family.

For four years they did their best, treating him like one of their own children. Family time, hard work, and loving discipline were a normal part of every day. When he didn't respond as the rest of their children did, they did the only thing they knew to do—the same thing they would have done with any of their own children. They treated him as a strong-willed child who needed a firm hand. They knew little about helping a child who was emotionally traumatized from a troubled past. Thinking he was just unruly, they hoped that a secure family, discipline, love, and time would solve the behavioral issues.

When Delmar ran away, they were shocked and deeply hurt. He was returned to the welfare system, but they lost touch with him after that. They would later find out that he had run away at five years of age before he had ever entered their home, so it wasn't the first time. Somehow this didn't ease the pain in Judy's heart. She had loved him as her own, and losing him had broken her heart and made her feel like a failure. The fact that he ran away the summer after Leonard's death made it even more painful. Now, to consider taking in another child like this, even though it was years later, stirred up a great deal of fear and uncertainty in her.

In the end, though, after much prayer and deliberation, they decided to take Marco in and give him a family. He came to live with them on July 3, 2003.

On the first evening in his new home, Marco looked at Dennis with wistful pleading in his dark eyes and announced, "I have to call you Daddy, because wherever I am, I need to call the man of the house Daddy."

"That will be just fine, Marco." Dennis smiled. He had a father's heart for the little neighbor boy, and it appeared that God had orchestrated that bond to prepare them for what He had in store.

From the beginning Marco had a heart for animals. "May I have a jar, Esther?" he begged one day.

"What for, Marco?" Esther lifted her hands from the sudsy dishwater and turned toward her foster brother.

"For my fish. Please? I want to keep them as pets." His pale face was eager with pleading, and Esther couldn't resist him. She found a small container for him and watched him scurry off to acquire his finned creatures. For many days he enjoyed watching them swim, and when they died, he replaced them with a baby duck in a cage and later a tiny bird.

Though the rest of the family was very involved in his life, Marco's hero was Dennis. Every moment of attention Dennis could spare for him was eagerly soaked up. "Tell me more, Daddy. Tell me more!" he would plead during the Bible stories at night. He sat enthroned on Dennis's lap, drinking in every word, his eyes riveted on his daddy's face as he listened to the stories of heroes of the faith, such as Joseph, Daniel, and the three young men in the fiery furnace.

After Bible stories they would romp and play on the floor together. Marco would jump astride Dennis's broad back with a delighted grin on his face and ride round the room like a Tico on his horse. Or they would start one of their tickling matches, and his boyish giggles would echo through the house mingled with Dennis's booming laughter.

There was much for Marco to learn in his new home, and it didn't all come easily for him. "Can I sleep in my clothes tonight?" he would ask plaintively. For weeks in a row he asked Dennis every night. The idea of pajamas had never been a part of his little boy routine, and he couldn't wrap his mind around why one needed separate clothes for night and day time. However, Dennis's firm and patient insistence every night that he needed to change from his dirty play clothes to his clean pajamas won out, and he finally quit asking.

Another point of adjustment was food. He was thin and pale when he came to them, perhaps from stress and poor eating habits. Esther's sisterly heart overflowed in planning ways to put weight on him, and he soon flourished, his cheeks filling out and growing rosy with health. It took several months to cure him of grumbling over the food and picking at things he didn't like, but he eventually learned to eat what was on his plate.

"Rebecca, I have a headache," he complained one afternoon in school. Rebecca was teaching in their church school that year, and it proved a prime opportunity for someone from the family to help Marco make this adjustment into a classroom setting.

It was not unusual for him to have headaches and tummy aches with all the stress of adjusting, but he was not beyond using it to his advantage either. "I'm sorry, Marco. You may get a drink of water if you think that would help, but then you need to concentrate on your school work, okay?"

A pout clouded Marco's face. He slouched in his seat.

"Marco, you need to have a cheerful attitude when you are asked to do something," Rebecca corrected firmly. He sat up straighter, but refused to pick up his pencil and get back to work.

"Marco, I'll need to discipline you if you don't obey and continue your studies as you've been told." Rebecca was happy to help with Marco's training, but she often felt in over her head, especially this afternoon. Only earlier in the week she had thought he was improving.

"I find myself praying so often for wisdom and love," she had told Esther the day before. "It helps, though, when there are no other students there to complicate the situation. And usually there aren't, since Marco only comes in the afternoons for his tutoring. I can tell he is slowly learning to sit and concentrate on studies."

Perhaps Rebecca wouldn't have been quite as stern if Marco's behavior earlier in the afternoon hadn't been so sour. But when Rosy dragged him up the hill to the schoolhouse, breathless from the struggle and put out by his stubbornness, Rebecca had been put on her guard. With a dark look, Marco yielded and finished his work, albeit carelessly. *I'll withhold any further scolding or punishment,* Rebecca decided. *He's only learning.* If it had been one of her other students, he would have received greater consequences.

That evening when Dennis heard that Rosy had needed to half-drag him up the hill to school, he had a serious talk with his foster son. "Don't let it happen again," he warned soberly.

Marco's weekly telephone calls with his birth mom, Evita, were another sore spot. He struggled in his child's mind to reconcile his two worlds and all the emotions that simmered up when he was reminded of his old life with her. The Kropfs were concerned about her influence in his life and kept the calls closely monitored, which Marco resented.

"I just can't wait for the day," Marco dreamed aloud, weeks ahead of the anticipated date. "The day my mama comes for my tenth birthday will be so wonderful! She always tells me about the presents she'll bring and the way she can't wait to help me celebrate. I know she misses me." His words held longing and hope.

Marco's birthday dawned bright and clear. As the car crunched into the lane, Marco threw open the house door and rushed out to meet his mother.

"Hello, Marco," Evita greeted momentarily as her son tried to hug her. She brushed a hand carelessly over his black hair.

"Did you bring gifts, Mama?" Marco's eyes shone with excitement.

"Let's go inside." Evita swung her purse carelessly over one arm and handed Marco a small, cheap bag of candy. "Here's your gift."

As they walked to the house, Marco's hungry eyes searched her face. She smiled at him briefly. "How long can you stay? I've missed you," he whispered longingly.

"A few hours. I'm busy these days." Her words held little warmth. During the rest of the visit, she hardly took notice of him. As she drove away, Marco kicked the dust dejectedly and rubbed his eyes hard. The ache inside him wouldn't go away for a long, long time.

His foster family did their best to make up for this emptiness in his heart. One day Dennis took him to San José when he had to do business there. They went out to eat for lunch, and Marco loved his hamburger. But it wasn't the food that mattered. It was the love that it represented that made the difference in his starving heart.

Rebecca expressed the family's feelings about their new addition in a piece of poetry she scribbled one day soon after he came.

> They sought him not—God brought him to their door.
> He needs a home, and options are no more.
> Frail humans cannot comprehend the heart that God doth fill.
> Would you have guessed the answer? By God's grace we will.

By God's grace they would do their best to fill Marco's life and heart with the love he craved, so that in time he would open his heart to the greatest love of all, the love of God. The family had no inkling of the shadow that lurked in the future for Marco and his uncle José, a shadow that would darken their world with immeasurable pain.

5

Let the Little Children Come

The baby wailed pitifully. Unshed tears welled up in Rebecca's eyes as she watched him lying in his hospital bed. Sweat stood out in beads on his dark skin, and the salty liquid trickled into his eyes. The family had grown to love Anderson in the last two months as they waited for him to get well enough to come home.

The call from the social worker had come unexpectedly. Another family in the area who did foster care had asked the Kropfs to be backup help for them. The welfare department had done a home study for that purpose. Time elapsed and they weren't called on to help their friends, so they hadn't expected the welfare department to pursue their family as a candidate for official long-term foster care. But that is what happened.

After praying and asking their ministry for advice, they had agreed to add Anderson to their family, in addition to Marco, who had been with them for two years by this time. Rebecca, Esther, and Rosy, who by now were in their mid to upper twenties, rejoiced at the decision. They hungered for more far-reaching ministry opportunities, more purpose and meaning in their lives as single women still living at home.

"Sometimes I long for a husband and a family of my own," Esther confided to Rebecca one afternoon. "But having a baby in the house again will be a way to fulfill some of that desire to nurture little ones, I think."

Rebecca nodded. "Someone once told me that even in singlehood we are meant to 'mother' those around us, because as women, we are created to nurture life. Whether that is on a physical or spiritual level and whether it's our own families or those who need a family and have none, I really think it's an inherent part of how God designed us. I've often felt the same ache for a family to call my own just like you have. Sometimes I want it so much, but I have to yield it back to God once again. I want to be open to however God chooses to orchestrate my life and how He chooses to weave my story with the story of those around me."

"I do too," Esther mused. "I think of Anderson's story and how God chose to bring him to us."

The baby had a sad history. Born to a thirteen-year-old Indian mother, Anderson had contracted meningitis at six months of age. He was airlifted to the San José Children's Hospital on life support. By the time the infection was finally under control, a large amount of damage had already been done. The lively, normal baby boy was now severely handicapped both mentally and physically, including blindness and partial paralysis. His needs were beyond his mother's scope of care. He had been in the hospital two months when the welfare department called the Kropfs and asked if they would take him in.

Esther and her father made the first trip to the hospital to see him. Learning to care for him came naturally for Esther. Quick, capable, yet tender, she had all the makings of a nurse. This gifting served her well as she learned how to use a feeding tube, how to know if it was displaced, how many feedings were needed, how much to feed, what medications he was on, what dosages to give, and what to expect with his present condition and limitations.

Then he contracted chickenpox and ended up in the intensive care unit. Time dragged. Now as Rebecca looked down at his poor little head, flattened from lying in bed so long, and his misery-etched face, she longed to cuddle him close and comfort away the pain and abandonment he must have been feeling. "If only you can get well enough to come home, little Andy Boy," she murmured as she touched his face and hands. As she walked away, she looked back longingly. "It seemed almost a sin to leave him alone for another night," she told Rosy later that evening.

Finally the day they had anticipated so long arrived. On May 16, 2005, the girls hurried all morning, cleaning the house till it shone. Rebecca came home early from teaching school. The white crib they had purchased stood in readiness with its blankets and mosquito net.

By three in the afternoon, the nurse and social worker who were bringing Anderson still hadn't arrived. Rebecca and Rosy decided they would milk the cows early so they would be done with everything and be free to enjoy the baby when he came. Even so they waited some time before the ambulance finally arrived.

Judy's sister, Aunt Ellen, and her husband, Uncle Richard, who lived several hours away, were there waiting with the family. Judy and Aunt Ellen went to the kitchen to make the customary cheese bread—bread with white cheese—and coffee for the guests when they arrived. The Costa Rican cultural norm of offering food to guests had become a natural part of welcoming people into their home.

Rebecca stood back and watched, silent tears flowing down her face as she watched the long-awaited bundle being carried into their living room. Esther greeted the nurse and social worker. Since she was the one who had learned the care procedures in the hospital, the nurse addressed her to explain new developments and details of the baby's therapy.

Meanwhile, when Judy came back from the kitchen, the social worker sat down with her and Dennis. Aunt Ellen and Rebecca soon joined them and found that they were discussing a rare disease called maple syrup urine disease (MSUD). "It's a rare genetic disorder," the social worker explained briefly. "We have a four-month-old baby named Diego who needs a home. He's an Indian baby from the Talamanca Mountains. He has mild brain damage, but this may be reversible. The parents aren't willing to do what it takes to get him back, so we are classifying him as abandoned. We wondered if you might be interested in caring for him."

"What kind of care does he require with this specific illness?" Rebecca asked with interest.

"MSUD is caused by a deficiency of enzymes required to metabolize certain amino acids in the body. Because these amino acids are not broken down, they accumulate in an abnormal way in the various cells and fluids of the body. This causes a variety of symptoms including poor appetite, lethargy, a lack of proper muscle function, and as its name implies, urine that carries the scent of maple syrup. It can even lead to seizures that, if left untreated, can cause brain damage.

"The good news is that the disorder is quite manageable if a patient is kept on a highly specialized diet. There is still risk of metabolic crises with sudden spikes in amino acid levels, and these require immediate medical help. But overall, a child can live a relatively normal life depending on how much damage is done before the disease is treated," the social worker explained carefully. She paused expectantly before adding, "We could bring him out tomorrow if you are willing."

Judy and Dennis exchanged wide-eyed glances with Rebecca and Aunt Ellen. "We can't say yes today." Dennis's tone sounded final. "We will have to think about it before taking on another child."

"I understand, but do think about it," urged the social worker. "I'll call you tomorrow and touch base about it."

The next day she called. "Could you give me a definite answer by Monday?"

Dennis glanced at the calendar. It was Tuesday. That would give them nearly a week to decide. "Yes," he told her.

The family presented it to their church body. "Is there another family that feels God leading them to give the baby a home?" Dennis asked the group. When no one else came forward, the Kropf family decided to say yes to little Diego.

That first week with Anderson, who was soon known as Andy, was packed with adjustments. With all his health issues, he required much more care than a normal baby. Even with three girls to share the feedings, it seemed they could hardly keep up with the schedule. But what was really difficult was listening to his crying.

He would cry for hours on end, all through the night and parts of every day. His sad, pitiful wail wore on the nerves and hearts of his new foster family until they felt raw from sleep deprivation and emotional weariness. By the close of the third day, they had nearly reached the end of their endurance.

In desperation, Esther called the nurse and asked if there was anything that could be done to make him comfortable. "Well, I can prescribe him some drops for pain, but otherwise you'll have to learn to ignore it. It's just a part of his condition," she told the anxious foster mother matter-of-factly. With time they learned that positioning him certain ways, such as helping him sit up and burp, seemed to ease his discomfort a little. And cruel as it seemed to them at first, they did adjust to the crying. It just became a part of the background noise in the hum of their home life.

Just before supper on a rainy Monday evening two weeks later, Marco announced that two vehicles were driving in the lane. After waiting all afternoon, the whole family was eager to meet little Diego. When the social worker placed him in Judy's arms, it was love at first sight. His round olive face and bright black eyes peeped out above fuzzy folds of the little blanket in which he was wrapped. He stared wide-eyed at all the people, alert and yet calm.

"May I hold him, Mama?" Esther held out eager arms.

"And me next." Rebecca smiled into the dark eyes of the new arrival. As they passed him from arm to arm, everyone oohed and aahed over how cute and precious he was. The personnel who had come to make the exchange watched closely as the family met and bonded with their newest addition, and they were pleased at what they saw. A doctor among them thoroughly explained MSUD and its possible complications, and a lab technician provided some additional information. Then, leaving him with their dad, the girls took the therapist into the baby's room to learn how to do therapy on both Andy and Arthur Dwight, which is what they had decided to name Diego. They thought they would call him by his middle name, Dwight.

They discovered they had been instructed wrongly about how to do Andy's therapy, and that he was regressing because of it. They were glad to relearn the proper way, and were even more pleased when he began to go from being stiff as a board to having movement in his limbs.

When they finished with the therapist, they came back out to the kitchen, and the nutritionist began to explain the feeding regimen for Dwight. Rebecca's mind spun with the number of details and the thought of another set of complicated feedings and therapy sessions. By now the other girls had abandoned her to enjoy the baby and care for Andy's needs, so she finished listening alone. When everything had finally been wrapped up, they served their guests cheese bread and coffee.

Looking at the group of professional caregivers, Rebecca asked, "How is this? Are there so many babies in the hospital that this baby won't even be missed, or do you notice his absence?" It was a question only Rebecca would think to ask.

The doctor answered for the group. "Oh, of course he'll be missed. You should see how the nurses have already suffered from seeing him leave. Especially with Diego; he was no one's baby—so I suppose he was everyone's baby."

"Oh! I'm sorry. That must be hard," Rebecca said.

"We are just happy to see them settled in a loving home," the group affirmed. The therapist who had been holding Andy during this conversation put him in his crib as they prepared to leave. Esther noticed that she was wiping tears from her eyes as she turned away from him. They left a bag of new clothes and baby things for Dwight when they left.

Later that evening as Rebecca was holding him she noticed that he had a bit of the same "hospital head" Andy had come with. Not nearly as severe, though. "We'll have to work on reshaping it," she told Esther, who was feeding Andy through his tube in the crib nearby.

"I noticed he doesn't know how to lay his head on your shoulder like a normal baby," Esther responded. "Even though the nurses love them, their work doesn't allow them a lot of time for holding babies. It's really heartbreaking when you think about it."

"Yes, his neck is a bit weak, but he'll develop fast now that he's getting lots of care in a home setting, I have no doubt." Rebecca cuddled him close, and her heart melted with a mother love she had never quite experienced before. "Welcome home, Dwightie," she crooned. His bright black eyes looked trustingly into hers, and she bent to kiss his downy head.

A few days after Dwight arrived, Rosy commented on how much he looked like Rebecca. It had been unofficially decided that Andy was Esther's baby and Dwight was Rebecca's. "The next one will be Rosy's baby," Rebecca declared.

Exhaustion badgered them as they trekked in and out of the emergency room with various health issues with baby Andy. When it was discovered that he was anemic, the doctor prescribed iron, and much to the whole family's relief, his crying fits nearly ceased! "Now he's awake and content for hours at a time." Esther stroked his downy head. "I'm so glad God gave us this answer to his health issues." At night he only cried in spurts now instead of crying most of the night.

Dwight grew fat and contented. Within the first week he had gained two pounds. At a doctor's appointment Rebecca broached the subject. "Dwightie is growing so fast. I'm wondering if it's healthy for him. Is there a way we could cut back on his feedings?"

The dark-haired pediatrician looked thoughtfully at the pudgy baby in front of him. Then he looked up with a slow smile. "He is a bit fat for his age. I'm sure your assessment is correct. Now that he's in a secure atmosphere with less stress, he doesn't need as much food."

Rebecca changed his feeding amounts accordingly, and his growth leveled out. Laughing fits at odd times had eased the girls through many of those tiring days, but now their bodies had a small chance to begin to catch up. However, it wasn't soon enough to spare them a severe attack of the flu that preyed on their sleep-deprived immune systems. Rosy was the first to succumb. She had been longing for rest and was also battling allergies. "Sometimes I almost wish I could get sick enough that I could just go to bed," she said one morning when she was feeling particularly unwell. But when she did get sick, she found it hard to rest because she felt so miserable!

On the second day both Rebecca and Marco came down with it. The babies contracted coughs, and Dwight ran a fever. Thankfully Judy had only a touch of it. Rebecca tried to go to school to teach after several days in bed, only to end up coming home early and crawling back in bed. Some of her pupils came to school with glassy eyes and hollow cheeks from their own bout with the serious virus. School was called off for six days, and coughs and weakness lingered on even after the worst of the illness was over.

One night Esther's best friend from church, Myrtle Bates, came to help care for the babies. Although sixteen-year-old Myrtle was several years younger than Esther, they shared a rare bond. Bold and strong but also deeply sensitive, both of them loved adventure and lived life at top speed, accomplishing much and finding fun around every corner. Myrtle's help and companionship proved to be a God-send during this time.

Several days and nights later a couple other girls from church came to carry the load. Without their help, caring for the infants, milking, chores, and household work would have been too much for the Kropf girls.

One Sunday soon after they had recovered from their bout of illness, they were sitting in church. Rebecca was empty-handed that Sunday as both babies were being held by the other girls. *I think we need another baby,* she thought to herself. *But maybe we should wait till after school is out. Then I won't be spending so much time helping Marco with his schoolwork, and I'll have more time to care for a baby full time. God, you know if it's right for us to have another baby, but it would seem so perfect if we'd have three.*

Both babies were in and out of the hospital a lot. Andy's convulsions had been growing worse and worse. They were slowly killing him, and he began to regress on his feeding and the physical progress they had made with his coordination and movement. Finally he was admitted to the hospital for a two-week stay until they could get his seizures under control. Esther remained faithfully at his side day and night, caring for him and watching over him as only a mother could.

It was during these two weeks that Rebecca's prayer for a third baby was answered. All the girls had been hoping that the next baby would be a girl, since Kenneth's family had four boys, and Michael, who was now married, had a boy as well. Being surrounded by little boys made them think about how much fun it would be to have a girl in their midst.

When they were introduced to a tiny baby girl with a severe skin disease, the nurses mentioned the possibility of them having her. A few weeks later the social worker called them, and the Kropf family asked the ministry for the third time in one year if they thought it was wise for them to take in yet another special-needs baby.

"You know your limits," came the calm response.

Esther and Rebecca went to the hospital and spent several days learning how to care for the little girl, and in December of 2005, Sandra Charlene came home to stay. Though tiny, Charlene was as feisty as a baby wild animal. She was also sensitive and took much longer to settle in than the first two babies had. But in time she became a lively little girl with dancing dark eyes and a temper that proved to the world that she knew exactly what she wanted and would do anything to get it. Rosy had her baby at last, and she loved her with all her heart.

A friend sent them a baby card with the words:

> Some would gather money along the path of life;
> Some would gather roses and rest from earthly strife,
> But I would gather children from among the thorns of sin;
> I would see a golden curl, and a freckled, toothless grin.
> For money cannot enter in the land of endless day,
> And roses that are gathered soon will wilt along the way,
> But oh, the laughing children, when I cross the sunset sea,
> And the gates swing wide to heaven; I can take them in with me.

In journaling about the joys and challenges of their new family, Rebecca wrote the following:

> "Inasmuch as ye have done it unto one of the least of these my brethren, ye have done it unto me" (Matthew 25:40). God speaks His will to us in many ways. When He asks something of us in a clear way, do we recognize it and respond, or do we ask as the interpreter of the law, "Who is my neighbor?" or "Who are the least of these?" God forbid . . . All this is in God's hand. From beginning to end, He brings it to pass. He knows where it will come, what all He wants us to do . . . "Jesus said, Suffer little children, and forbid them not, to come unto me: for of such is the kingdom of heaven" (Matthew 19:14).

6

A Troubled Soul

Rebecca plunged another load of dirty laundry into the sudsy water swishing in the wringer washing machine. Marco sneaked around the corner, and with a look of antagonism in his dark eyes, he quickly unplugged the power cord to the washer. Scurrying away, he looked back and noted that Rebecca had seen him. However, she didn't respond. She simply plugged in the washer and went on with her work, humming a hymn cheerfully.

Nonplussed and evidently frustrated, Marco came back a moment later and did the same thing. Three or four times the process was repeated, and every time Rebecca patiently ignored the aggressive behavior. As she plugged the cord in a fourth time, she failed to see an infuriated Marco rush at her with his fist raised. The blow to the side of her face made her see stars, and she staggered back.

"Marco!" she cried out in pain. Her twelve-year-old foster brother stood by with a dark look on his fair-skinned Costa Rican features. She held back tears. "We'll have to talk about consequences for this behavior, Marco.

You can't act like this, no matter how angry you feel."

In the three years since Marco had come to them, he had begun to exhibit increasing amounts of anger and aggression. At first they had applied consequences and given him more chores to do. Rebecca tried to help him express his fears and frustrations in a safe environment. She started a notebook for him, asking him why he was angry or sad on a regular basis and writing his thoughts down on paper. In this way she hoped to give him a safe place to express his anger without his taking it out on those around him.

"Today I was angry at Esther," he declared one afternoon during their talk time. "She was watching me work in the garden, and I had already done what she told me to do, but she looked to make sure anyway." He had a fair number of verbal clashes with Esther because of her outspoken personality and her drive for doing things right and getting things done.

Another day he admitted he had been frustrated, but he said, "I prayed for help and thought about Scripture this morning, and it seemed to help me overcome my anger. Later, though, I didn't want help, and I just felt angry again."

When few of their efforts seemed to bring any lasting fruit, they ceased using physical punishment altogether. They agreed that it just seemed to stir up his anger more.

Unfortunately, it wasn't until this aggressive behavior had become ingrained in Marco that the Kropfs began to understand how deeply he had been traumatized by the abuse and neglect he had experienced in his early childhood. This trauma made it difficult for him to trust his foster parents and siblings, and crippled his ability to process his negative emotions in healthy ways. Instead, he vented his rage and pain through aggression and destructive behavior toward others.

As the family gained more knowledge of the unique needs of children like this, they began to adapt their training style accordingly, setting up a system of natural consequences to punish his behavior, while working on establishing trust, respect, and personal responsibility. They responded to his attempt to gain power through negative behaviors by allowing natural consequences to take their course and by refusing to react in anger. But by now Marco's character was not as malleable as it once had been; even this new approach to training proved insufficient to curb his rebellion.

The violent episodes continued. One day when he was out in the yard with Judy, he started throwing wood from the woodshed at her. Because of her heart condition, Judy was on a blood thinner, and Rebecca knew it was dangerous for her to get any sort of bleeding injury. With this in mind, she rushed outside and grabbed her younger brother from behind. No one else was home to help, but he was small, and she restrained him effectively without hurting him, though he struggled violently against her strong grasp.

From where he lay on the ground, he continued to fight her, yelling angrily at the top of his lungs. "Marco, listen to me!" she shouted above his yelling. "I have something to say to you." For a moment he stilled, and she looked into the misery-filled eyes set in his light brown face. Catching her breath a little from the struggle, she told him, "I don't think this is the way God wants you to be. I'll let you go, but you have to know that this behavior is not okay. It is not okay to hurt Mama." She let him go, and he calmed down. After that he never attacked Mama again.

Sometimes when there were no natural consequences, they had to create their own. If he acted out verbally, they might ask him to sit with his hand over his mouth in silence until he could speak kindly. If he hurt someone, he might have to give up his pet rabbit and earn it back with time, because if he was hurting people, he couldn't be trusted to take care of a helpless animal. Slowly they worked with him to try and bring structure and logic to how he thought through behavior and consequences. It was hard on all of them, especially since they had other needy children to care for as well.

He wasn't always angry, though. There were still many moments when his tender heart showed through. It seemed that perhaps he had finally bonded enough to begin to let his anger diffuse and to find the boundaries of safe emotions within family relationships. His foster family prayed fervently that in time he would normalize and become a settled adult.

Despite his behavior and moods, Marco always seemed to adore Dennis. One day in January he was down working by the bridge, and Dennis went down to help him. Dennis stepped on a rock and it rolled from under him. As he went down, his leg snapped. Dennis was a big man, and Marco felt helpless and scared when he saw his hero on the ground, white with pain. He ran for help. It took six men to get Dennis out.

"Daddy's not young anymore. I hope his leg will heal." Rebecca's forehead creased with worry.

Marco burst into tears.

"He will heal, won't he?" he inquired desperately.

"He'll heal, Marco," Rosy comforted. "Don't cry. It will be okay. He's a strong man."

"And we can pray for him, okay?" Rebecca added, giving him a hug. Marco nodded and brushed a tear away with the back of his hand.

7

Runaway

Associating with his uncle and friend José, however, began to have a negative influence on Marco as they grew older. José's attitude had grown increasingly perverse toward authority and life in general. Marco did have some desire to do right, but he found it easier to choose the lower path than to choose the straight and narrow path of God. He also chose not to respond to the voices of authority and the Holy Spirit in his life. The older the two became, the more mischief they got into. Sometimes Dennis considered cutting off Marco's contact with José altogether as he saw these worrisome trends developing.

One Sunday the avalanche that had been building for months was unleashed by one small event. Marco, who was plenty old enough to understand what it meant to be reverent in church, was turning around and smirking at José, who was fooling around and making faces. When he didn't listen to Dennis's quiet rebuke and continued to turn around and be disruptive, Dennis acted on impulse.

"Marco, if you are going to keep looking back, you can just stand up and face José. Stand up right now." It wasn't optional. It was a command. Marco knew he had been beaten. Red with shame, he stood up and faced the back of the church for several moments while the service went on around him. Then Dennis let him sit back down.

At the end of the service a Costa Rican brother approached Dennis. "Do you really think that was the right way to handle that situation? It didn't seem quite right to me to publicly shame him," he warned quietly.

On the way home from church Dennis was thoughtful. "Rebecca, do you think I acted out of turn by how I disciplined Marco in church today?" he asked with concern. Since his wife hadn't been there, he asked his oldest daughter's opinion.

"I don't think it was right," Rebecca admitted quietly.

"I guess I acted without thinking it through," Dennis humbly acknowledged. "Sometimes I just don't know how to handle his behavior. He seems to get worse and worse."

"We'll have to keep praying for a breakthrough soon," Rebecca agreed.

The next day Marco ran away. The thirteen-year-old made his way down through the field and left the farm by a roundabout track. When the family realized he was missing, they contacted the welfare department to let them know what had happened on Sunday and that it seemed Marco had run away because of the incident. They didn't pursue him personally, though. If he wanted to, he would come back in his own time. Forcing him would do little good at his age.

"The house is just achingly sad," Rebecca said to her sisters. "But in some ways it's strange how relieving the silence is. I feel guilty admitting to feeling that way, but it's true. I worry about Marco, but it's been so draining to have these constant battles in our home."

"I agree." Esther busied herself with making afternoon coffee as she spoke. "I worry about him every time I turn around, and it's been almost three days now. But at the same time, my soul is soaking in the quiet."

Rosy said nothing, but nodded in understanding as she brooded over her cup of dark coffee.

As the family prayed for their wayward son, Dennis's mind went to a scene from Marco's childhood, on a day eight years earlier when José was staying with them for a short visit. Dennis had been working in the field near the pond when he caught sight of the two five-year-olds near the water's edge. "Boys, don't get too close to the edge. You could fall in."

"Okay!" two little voices had responded in unison.

Dennis turned his concentration back to his work.

"Can you swim?" José eyed the pond appraisingly.

"I'm going to someday." Marco's pensive black eyes followed his playmate's gaze.

"Not today, though. He thinks it's dangerous." José glanced over his shoulder at Dennis's broad back, then turned and threw a mud ball bouncing into the water. "Let's go out to the end of the dock," he suggested.

They ran over the warm gray boards of the dock. Suddenly Marco tripped. Before he had time to cry out, the dark water rushed up to greet him.

Splash!

Dennis had turned just in time to see the small form disappear under the water. José let out a cry of fear and ran to peer over the edge of the dock where his playmate had fallen in. In a few hurried strides Dennis was beside him. He reached out a large hand and caught Marco by the shirt, dragging him up out of the water and into his arms. Coughing and sputtering, the little boy clung to him, water running in rivulets from his soaked clothes and hair.

"Are you okay, Marco?" Dennis set the boy on his feet on dry ground and knelt beside him.

Marco rubbed water out of his eyes and nodded, sniffling.

"Didn't I tell you boys not to go near the water?" Dennis asked.

Both boys hung their heads and nodded. "Go to the house and get dry clothes."

Neither boy knew the love of a father. Dennis was the closest thing they had known.

Later that night when the two little figures knelt beside their beds to pray their bedtime prayer, Marco had prayed, "Thank you for the big man who saved me from the water."

How desperately Marco needed a rescue now! This time the dark waters of sin and rebellion threatened to overpower him. If only he could reach out to the strong arms of the Father who longed to save him from destruction!

On the fourth day welfare personnel found him at a relative's house. They asked him if he would like to come back to his foster family's home to talk things through. He came with them quietly, and after they had visited with the family, they went and got him from the pickup truck where he had been sitting and waiting.

Rebecca watched from the porch, praying inwardly for grace for her parents as they went out to stand near the truck. With downcast eyes the boy approached them.

Dennis's eyes filled with tears as he bent down and pulled him into a strong hug. Marco received it willingly, and tears spilled over and coursed down his cheeks.

In a choked voice Dennis asked, "Can you forgive me? That wasn't the right way to handle that situation, and I was wrong."

Marco nodded wordlessly, and when his dark eyes met Dennis's blue ones, they both knew things had been made right.

But Marco didn't choose to stay. The turmoil inside him pushed him to expand his horizons and find his own way. He chose to go back to his birth family despite its dysfunctions. For years to come he would still call Dennis "Daddy" and treat the Kropfs with the familiarity of family. José, however, seemed determined to lead the way on a downward spiral toward evil. The troubled church community could only watch and pray. One of the many heart-rending questions in their future would be whether José would have been willing to turn and accept God's love while still young, had he known the depths of evil that the forces of darkness would lead him into in the years ahead.

The Kropfs continued to show Marco love whenever they got the chance. They were quick to admit that they were imperfect and had made mistakes. But they had also deeply loved him and given him all the care and help they knew how to give, opening their hearts, home, and time to his need. Despite the scars in their hearts from that season of wrestling to love and guide Marco, they prayed for him often. "Lord," Rebecca often whispered into the darkness beside her bed, "someday let Marco know that the love of the Father in heaven is enough to bring healing to his hurt and hope to his struggle. Help him find you, heavenly Father, and freedom for his troubled soul."

8

A Baby Boom

"I'm worried about Charlene's eye," Rosy told Rebecca one Sunday. "She's so miserable and it's worse than usual." With her epidermolysis bullosa—also known as butterfly disease—Charlene frequently developed blisters and open wounds on her delicate skin. She was at constant risk for infection, but the ulcers that formed in her eyes seemed to be particularly painful.

"She does look bad," Rebecca said. "Let's keep praying about it."

That afternoon as they all sat around the kitchen table reading and writing letters, Charlene, her usually sparkling black eye bandaged to protect it from light, sat at the table beside Rosy. The infection and pain had sapped much of her normal two-year-old energy, and she was unusually still and quiet.

Rosy glanced at her little girl and then reached out to cradle Charlene's head and place it in her lap. As she did so, she heard Charlene utter the words, "Jesus, make Lenie better."

Quick tears came to Rosy's eyes as she heard the simple prayer. "Did you hear that, Rebecca?" she asked softly. Rebecca nodded. Rosy could just picture the father heart of God stirring with special interest at this small but faith-filled request.

By that evening Charlene was already improving. The next morning when she woke up, she was able to open her eyes to the light without nearly as much pain. A short time later when they visited the eye specialist, there was not even a scar where the terrible ulcer had been. Jesus had answered her prayer. How He must have delighted in her childlike faith!

The stretching and joys of raising children with special needs filled the Kropf home with challenges and laughter. Three years had slipped by since they had taken in their first foster baby, and they had slowly adjusted to their new lifestyle. Some things became so natural that they did them in their sleep. Rebecca and Esther were getting breakfast during a cousin's visit one morning when the cousin laughingly brought this truth home. "Esther, what were you trying to do last night?" she asked as she came into the kitchen. "I woke up twice to you patting me like a baby."

Esther's eyes widened in surprise. Rebecca burst out laughing.

"I guess I've gotten so used to calming Andy in my sleep that I do it without even waking up!" Esther joined the laughter.

Some of the more major adjustments came with learning to handle having the children in and out of the hospital so much and learning to cope with socialized medical care. They always used private hospitals for their own health care; socialized medical care tended to be lower quality and more impersonal, which took some adjusting. Often they found it necessary to advocate for their babies because they knew their children and knew what was needed. The medical personnel did their best, but sometimes they were too removed from the situation or too busy to really notice or realize what was happening.

Esther's strong personality serves her well as she fights for the needs of her children, Rebecca reflected as she took another shirt from the pile of crumpled laundry and smoothed it over the ironing board. She thought back to the way Esther's determination to have things done right had come into play in caring for Andy over the past several weeks. After the doctor put Andy on heavy medication for his seizures, his gums started growing. One of the drugs produced this side effect, and eventually his gums grew so large that it became difficult for Esther to care for him. The doctors decided to surgically remove the overgrown gums, and Andy was admitted to the children's hospital in San José for the procedure. When she kissed him goodbye before the surgery, she prayed silently for God's hand over his little life.

After the surgery Andy wouldn't stop bleeding. Esther stayed on the fourth floor as the long hours crept by and her boy didn't come out of recovery. She could see through the partially opened door that they had to keep suctioning blood, and the deposit container was half full of bloody water. "I ache to go to him. Just to touch him and tell him it's going to be okay," Esther murmured to herself. "But I can't even promise him that it will be okay—even if I could be with him." She moaned inwardly, fighting the anguish that welled up inside.

The halls of the fourth floor were cold and drafty, and a chill wind blew as night fell over the capital city. Esther huddled on a bench. Her toes curled in her stockings as the cold seeped through her. Every little while she would go peek through the cracked door to check on Andy. "God, please help my baby. He needs you and I can't go to him." Hot tears coursed down her cheeks as she shifted on the cold, hard bench, trying in vain to sleep. At last she drifted into a troubled sleep, shivering as the cold, weary night dragged on.

Finally Andy came out of recovery and was admitted to the intensive care unit. During those long hours of fighting to control the bleeding in the cold recovery room, he had caught pneumonia as he so easily did. He had to wear a respirator, and his breathing came in ragged gasps. Esther was only allowed in for ten minutes every four hours. When she first saw him after surgery, she held his hand and cried tears of relief.

For a week Andy fought for his life, and Esther visited him and prayed for him around the clock, sleeping and eating haphazardly in between. She wouldn't let anyone else distract her, though she kept in touch with the family at home frequently throughout each long day.

The nurses cared for him carefully and attentively, but not the therapist, who came to ensure that Andy didn't get bedsores. He handled the child roughly, and after one of his visits Esther found Andy's respirator mask in his eyes. It had rubbed them raw. Something in Esther snapped. Suffering was one thing. Needless suffering was another. Andy had enough to deal with without being at the mercy of careless hands!

Contacting the nurse, Esther notified her of the situation. Later she was sent to ophthalmology. "You need to take better care of his eyes. You need to be more careful," the technician scolded her, unaware of the situation. Provoked by the frustration she still felt at the unneeded suffering of her child, she couldn't handle being blamed for it. She replied rather tartly, "It happened here at the hospital, sir."

"It couldn't have happened here. This is a sign of inexperienced care," the tech responded.

"No, sir, it was the therapist who was careless when he came to turn him in the ICU," Esther insisted firmly. "I think we need a different therapist to care for him. I don't want my baby to have to suffer needlessly." Finally they grudgingly acknowledged her explanation. After putting ointment in his eyes and covering them with thick gauze, he was returned to intensive care. It was another week before he had stabilized enough for Esther to bring him home. It was a miracle he had pulled through at all, considering how ill he had been. But the experience had taken its toll, and Esther had to choose to forgive more than once in those two long weeks.

When the call came about another baby boy who needed a home,

Dennis, Judy, and Rebecca went to see him. "We just need a short-term placement for him, maybe four months or so," the social worker explained.

Rebecca, curious what his name was, thought, *What if it would be Gerald?* It was one of her favorite names, but she knew it was rather ridiculous to guess. When they arrived at the hospital, she was more than a little surprised to find out that the child's name was Gerald!

"You can take him in about a week," they were told. He had an enterostomy, where his small intestine had been rerouted to an opening in his abdomen. They were about to remove the enterostomy tube, and after that he would be ready to be placed.

During the same time, the children's hospital contacted them about taking two little girls. They were sisters, named Selena and Kimberly. They had a debilitating genetic handicap, which caused many seizures, a vegetative physical state, and severe mental disabilities. Their unwed mother had been only thirteen when her first child was born. Now at the ages of two and five, the girls had been completely abandoned.

"How many children do you feel we can handle? You girls are the ones who shoulder most of the physical care." Dennis continued the discussion that had threaded through many dinner table and living room conversations while the home studies were being done. "There is also the question of which children are best suited to our family. Some children may fit better than others."

"I think we can handle several more children," Esther said confidently. Her can-do attitude had a way of rubbing off on others.

"It's really hard to say no when we don't know if these children will ever be in a Christian home if we don't take them," was Rebecca's input.

Then Gerald's surgery ended in complications, and he was not ready to come to them right away. Rebecca began to wonder if they would get him at all.

Another call came soon after for Dwight's sister. Her name was Karla, and she was another MSUD case. She was living in a children's home, and because they didn't have the personnel or the time to care for her properly, she needed to find another place to live. "We want to place her in a home where she will receive the long-term care she needs to thrive," the social worker said.

Two days passed, and they received no new word on Gerald. "I can't understand why social services hasn't contacted us about him," Rebecca worried to Esther. "The pediatrician in the hospital said he should be back by this time for sure."

"Call the hospital and check on him," Esther replied briskly.

"Why didn't I think of that? You're always the proactive one, Esther." Rebecca reached for her cell phone and dialed the number.

"He's in very grave and delicate condition," the medical staff informed her.

"I have to go to him," Rebecca told Esther when she hung up. "The mother in me can't stand by any longer." That Thursday she got permission, and the following day she went to visit him. She showed her permission papers to be admitted, and when she found Gerald's crib, she was shocked to see how he had deteriorated. He was dreadfully thin with a greatly swollen abdomen, and he was crying pathetically. A male nurse stood by his crib trying to feed him a bottle.

After a few moments of chatting about his condition and Rebecca's interest in taking him in as a foster child, Rebecca asked the nurse, "May I hold him?"

The man surveyed Rebecca warily. "My mother once cared for a child for four months, and it was awful. I don't advise you to do it."

"I'm not concerned about that. But may I hold him?" Rebecca persisted.

"If you wish," the nurse relented, "but I wouldn't take him home if I were you."

A rocker sat by each bed in the pediatric ward. Scooping the crying child up in her arms, Rebecca sank into the rocker and pulled Gerald close. He could hardly drink any milk at all before his tummy would distend, and he would cry and cry. Rebecca burped him and fed him tiny amounts, all the while rocking him. The motion and touch seemed to calm him.

Since the doctors were saying he could probably go home by Monday, she asked if she could just stay the weekend. She was granted permission, and she settled back into the rocker. All through that long night she held and bonded with Gerald. He calmed to her touch and love. By the end of that first long day and night, he clearly recognized her voice, and she loved him.

Gerald had been born to a poor family from Panama who lived in Costa Rica. He was the ninth child and the second of twins. Because they were Panama Indians and not Costa Rican citizens, the government always sent them back across the border for the birth of their children. When Gerald was born, they had to leave him in the hospital in Panama for a month and a half before they were allowed to bring him back to Costa Rica with them where they lived. After only two weeks at home, his enterostomy site got infected, and he was taken to a hospital in Costa Rica, where he spent a lot of time alone. His mother had the care of the normal twin and all her other children, and though she often visited him, she was limited in how much she could do.

In the end the Kropf family took all four of the children they had been considering. Kimberly would become Esther's little girl, and Selena would be considered Rosy's. Rebecca would take charge of Karla and Gerald. And though they didn't guess it then, all four of the children would be placed in their home long-term and grow up as part of the family.

On the happy day when Rebecca brought Gerald home, Dwightie, who was now a toddler, was kneeling beside the new baby on the bed. Suddenly he exclaimed, "Baby Zeral smiling." Sure enough, when Rebecca looked, Gerald was smiling up into Dwightie's grinning face.

Sweeping the toddler off the bed into a happy hug, Rebecca asked,

"Does my Dwightie like the new baby?"

Dwightie giggled and nodded. Rebecca hugged him to her heart "I'm so glad God made me your mommy," she told the little boy. "I feel thankful for you every day!" She kissed him again, and his bright eyes twinkled merrily.

"Tickle me, Mama." he begged, wriggling in her arms. She tousled his hair and tickled his chubby tummy. *How can you love this intensely someone you didn't give birth to?* she wondered. *God certainly has a unique way of making some of us mothers. He is a father to the fatherless. I guess He deeply values these little ones and knows how to open our hearts to His love for them.*

That month in 2008 had been a baby boom for them, and now their home was full and bursting at the seams with seven special children to love—Dwight, Andy, Charlene, Gerald, Karla, Kimberly, and Selena. It seemed there would never be a dull moment again. These needy children were claiming their places in the girls' hearts, but there remained an empty corner in each for Marco. They occasionally heard reports of his activities that showed his troubled search for fulfillment and a meaningful place in life, a search that was taking him to all the wrong places. A search that would ultimately lead him back to the family that was willing to keep loving through the worst he could bring them.

9

Bread of Tears

The Sunday morning service had been shattered by a commotion—Esther had fainted. In the chaos of the moment, Dennis and Kenneth came and carried her from the sanctuary. Andy's wheelchair had been overturned, and he hung upside down under the seat, wailing. One of the men came quickly to his aid and set him upright. Meanwhile, out on the veranda, Rebecca was doing all she knew to do to help Esther. The sisters had had their hands full with caring for their seven foster children over the past months. Now Esther's health needs added to the strain.

"These spells are becoming more than worrisome," Rebecca muttered to Rosy as she held a wet cloth to Esther's forehead.

"I know." Rosy fanned Esther's face. "These health issues just seem to be getting worse." Recently, after Esther had arrived home from a trip, Rebecca had been awakened during the night by the sound of Esther vomiting violently. "This is the third time I've thrown up tonight, and I'm so sick!" Esther fell weakly into bed. "These migraines are so horrible. I had one on my trip that went on and on, and now I am sick with another one."

"Esther, this is going so far that it's getting hazardous to your health. It's not safe for you to go anywhere by yourself. I think we need to start praying that God would reveal to us what is behind all this, because we need to deal with the root problem." Concern creased Rebecca's forehead. "Here, let me get you some electrolytes. I'll be right back."

They had been to the chiropractor and found that Esther's neck was severely out of place. Years before she had fallen from a horse headfirst. When she landed in the ditch, she had heard a crunching sound in her spine, but she had gotten up and gone on. They hadn't had access to a chiropractor at that time. Now that they did, Esther found relief from her migraines, although she still had milder ones from time to time.

But her health issues continued with breathless fainting spells that would come over her at odd times. After this incident in church, Esther felt utterly embarrassed that it had happened in public and that she had needed to be carried out. "How humiliating!" she groaned to Rosy.

"I just wish we could figure out what is causing them," Rebecca said. "I don't want you to die on us, Esther."

"Sometimes I feel almost as if I'm going to die." Esther sighed. "I feel so weak and breathless."

Esther and Rosy had each moved into their own houses with their children, making the main Kropf home a more restful place for their mother, whose health continued to decline. Rosy, Charlene, and Selena lived in the little house situated across the banana patch from the big house. Esther's little apartment, where she lived with Andy and Kimberly, took up one end of the shed across the yard from the main house. Esther loved having her own nest. She sewed lavender curtains for all the windows, and she loved serving up a cup of coffee in her cheery kitchen to anyone who came to visit. But even walking across the yard and up to the big house was enough to make her breathless and pale around the mouth these days.

She had to lean against the counter, breathing hard, until she regained her strength.

Sometimes she would black out. Often she felt dizzy and faint, and her hands would get stiff and cold. How they all wished they could solve this mystery! One Saturday morning when she was having another attack, Rebecca and Dennis decided to take her to the doctor in the middle of it so he could observe her. Unfortunately, the spell had passed by the time they reached the edge of town.

One day she had a particularly bad spell. Rosy and Rebecca were praying and doing all they knew to restore her. Her face was chalky, and her hands and feet were stiff and cold. She gasped for breath and didn't respond to them. "Lord Jesus, please help us," Rebecca prayed desperately.

Several moments later the attack passed, as they always did. But this one had seemed different. "I thought you were dying!" Rebecca told her in distress.

"I thought so too," Esther said. "Everything was going black, and I couldn't breathe. It felt different than my other fainting fits. I don't know how to describe it, but I was begging God not to let me die in front of Charlene and Karla."

With her driven personality and love for work, this health crisis tried Esther exceedingly. She wrestled with feeling helpless and having no answers, and she wrestled with fear of what others might think. The Psalms comforted her often. Sometimes she felt as if God was feeding her "the bread of tears" and "the water of affliction," as the Scriptures so aptly describe suffering.

But she clung to His words of promise, offering up the praise of faith even through the darkness of the unknown. Through her tears and struggles to trust, she found His comfort her mainstay.

Her many visits to the doctor revealed nothing. They tested her blood sugar levels and blood pressure various times at home in hopes of detecting something irregular. One doctor suggested that she was having stress attacks.

"I just can't accept that," Esther told Rosy. "Does he mean it's all from an emotional, not physical, cause? Do you think it's in my head?"

"I don't know, but I don't think so." Rosy put her arm around Esther's shoulder. "The chiropractic treatment helped your headaches a lot. There is probably a physical cause for your other symptoms too."

"Sometimes it feels almost hopeless." Esther sighed. How easy it was to get discouraged when her weakness dragged on and no answers came.

One day when Esther took her blood pressure, an irregular heartbeat showed up. When she showed the results to her father, he immediately called Judy's heart doctor. Esther had had rheumatic fever as a young child, and with Judy's history of heart trouble, Dennis was rightfully concerned over this irregularity. The appointment was set for the next day. "Maybe at last we'll find answers!" Esther's eyes looked hopeful as Dennis hung up the phone.

"It would be ideal if the doctor could see her during one of her attacks," Rebecca mused. "But I guess there isn't really any way we can arrange that, is there? We'll just have to keep asking God to reveal things as He wills."

When Dennis and Esther arrived at the hospital the next day, Esther told him, "I feel as if I would have an attack if I just climbed those few stairs."

Due to her weakened state, those six steps took all the breath and energy she possessed, just as she had predicted. Dennis helped her into a lobby chair, where she sat gasping for breath. A receptionist saw her, and when Dennis told them they were there for an appointment with the cardiologist, a nurse immediately brought a wheelchair and took her back to the cardiac department. There the doctor was quickly summoned.

"We need to take her in for an echocardiogram right away," the doctor said. "We'll also do an electrocardiogram."

When the results came back, he seemed mildly astonished. "She has a slight heart murmur and a mitral valve prolapse, but nothing is showing up that should be causing the kind of severe symptoms she is having. It could be something neurological. We'll order a CAT scan and an EEG to rule out seizures. Maybe that will reveal something we are missing."

After blood was drawn for a host of tests and the other scans had been done, Esther and Dennis went home. They waited hopefully for the results. When they came, the doctor said, "They're normal. Nothing is showing up. If you would like, we can order an MRI, but none of the other tests indicated anything that would make this necessary."

Esther had been saving money for a trip to the States for a family reunion. Almost everything she had saved had already been spent on tests and doctor visits. With her father's advice, they decided it would be best not to pursue more testing. "It could be that a psychologist or psychiatrist would help—if it would be something along that line," the doctor said kindly. Esther was mortified. She prided herself on being self-sufficient and capable, and the thought of weakness in any part of her life was difficult to swallow.

"I am just so sick of being sick and having doctors say it's all in my head," she wailed to Rebecca that night. "I just want to be well again. Is it really all in my head?" She held a cup of coffee between her chilled hands. "Look, I am so weak, I just shake, and I often feel so trembly in my core."

"I know, Esther. I mean, it could be stress. But I really don't think it is. We are not going to give up hope."

"And now I probably won't be able to go to the States to see the cousins and Michael's family." The seemingly endless pain, topped with another major disappointment, brought hot tears to Esther's eyes. "Nearly everything I had saved is gone with these medical bills. Sometimes I just want to cry and ask God, 'Why?' I wonder if I did something wrong or if there is something I just won't learn. What is wrong? It's not that I don't trust Him. I just don't understand."

The answer to their prayers came in an unexpected way. Rebecca was reading a natural health book one day when she came across a section on magnesium deficiency. "Daddy, doesn't this sound like Esther's condition?" she asked excitedly.

"It sure does!" His face brightened. "Tell her about it."

Later that day she read the section to Esther. "Doesn't it sound like what you're experiencing?" she asked.

"It does," Esther replied thoughtfully.

"You should at least try taking some magnesium and see if it helps," Rebecca said.

Within three days of starting on the supplement, Esther told Rebecca, "I think I can tell a difference. I can't be sure yet, but I am almost positive I feel stronger."

Within a week she could walk to the house without getting breathless. And she wasn't nearly as shaky. Slowly her symptoms began to fade, and her health began to come back. In His own time and way, God had given them the answers they sought. Though her health was still fragile, they praised God for the healing that had come. The great Physician was still in charge, and their lives were in His hands.

10
"Good Night, Dwightie"

"They are only giving her a twenty-percent chance to live," Rosy tearfully informed the family over the phone. Selena had been having such severe convulsions that her lungs had collapsed, and the doctors didn't think she would pull through this time. It was December 2008, and they'd had the seven foster babies for seven months now. The thought of losing one of them was hard.

During Selena's hospital stay, Rebecca was praying at home one day when little Dwight, now three, scampered in. "Mamita, I want to pray." His black eyes sparkled with life and energy.

"Okay, Dwightie, Mamita will help you pray." As his baby voice repeated a simple little prayer, Rebecca's mind flashed back to another recent event similar to this.

They had been at the beach as a family, and Rebecca had been resting in the van with a headache when Esther brought Dwightie to the van. When he saw Rebecca with her head down, he had asked, "Mamita sleeping?"

Esther, known as Tato to the children, replied, "No, she's a little bit sick.

Maybe you should say a prayer for her."

Without a moment's hesitation, the toddler had laid his chubby little hand on his mommy's forehead and prayed, "God is great, and God is good." Then after a moment, "Better now?" It had melted Rebecca's mommy heart!

Now as he finished praying he looked up at her with a happy smile. Rebecca hugged him tight against her and kissed his jet black hair. For a few moments they chatted, and then quite suddenly Dwightie announced, "Mamita, I want to go to Jesus."

"Yes, darling, when Jesus comes for us, we can go to Him." Rebecca remembered how she had just recently talked with Dwightie about the possibility of Selena going to heaven because she was so sick. *Precious little lamb,* she mused, *I didn't realize how much he would understand the concept of heaven. But he certainly does.*

· ·

"I wanna hold him, I wanna hold him!" Dwight pleaded as Rosy carried Andy down the hall. He ran ahead of Tía Woodsy (Rosy) on his short legs. Hopping onto the couch, he turned around and held out his chubby arms. Rosy looked down into sparkling black eyes with a smile. "You always want to hold the babies, don't you, Dwightie?" His energy and urge to explore and wander made him hard to keep track of. One evening he managed to get all the way out to the milk barn, and another time he wandered down to the dock by the pond. Tío Kenneth had sprinted down to retrieve him, but it had scared them all a little. They discussed ways of keeping him contained while he learned the basic boundaries of the farm, and they watched him closely whenever he was ouside.

The dew had settled on the grass early one evening when Rebecca, stirred by the loveliness of the weather, decided to take the children for a walk. With Gerald in one arm and Karla in the other, Dwight tagged along behind. Not too long later a little voice called out, "Mamita, me 'tuck." Sure enough, the little fellow had tangled his feet in some vines and couldn't get free. Rebecca's arms were tired, and they all turned back after she had freed little Dwight. As they wandered back through the tropical evening, Rebecca's heart swelled in gratitude to God for the beautiful gift of life. Each one of these children had become precious to her.

Later that same evening as Dennis, Kenneth, and Rebecca finished up the day's duties in the family-run bakery business they had established several years earlier, Rebecca sent three-year-old Charlene to the house. She was standing right behind her as the little girl stepped out onto the porch. Just then Rebecca saw something that made her heart jump into her throat. A deadly snake was poised to strike, coiled only a few paces ahead of Charlene. The child was heading straight for it.

Instantly Rebecca grabbed Charlene by the shoulders and lifted her off her feet, sweeping her back into the bakery. Shouting, she brought Dennis running to see what was going on. Charlene's black eyes widened with fear at this sudden, loud shift of events. She hadn't seen the snake, and she didn't understand. But Dennis saw it, and within moments the snake lay dead.

"That was a close call!" Rebecca was shaking with relief. "Praise God for His protection!"

The next day, a Saturday, began as any other day. Rebecca was up early before any of the children stirred. As she prepared for the day she prayed, "Lord, be with us in whatever this day holds."

Selena was still in the hospital after more than a week. The day before, Rosy had taken her by ambulance to another hospital to see a lung specialist. The doctor at the second hospital had said there was nothing they could do for her and had directed that she be taken back to the first one. Before they could do so, Selena began to convulse. When they couldn't seem to get it under control, the hospital staff finally decided to keep her overnight, and the ambulance left without her.

Rosy slept in a recliner, and for the first night in nine nights she slept hard. It had been a long vigil, and none of them knew when it would end, but God had given her good sleep to tide her through whatever might lie ahead. Esther was in the hospital with Kimberly as well, and Rebecca knew she would not get much work done that day—probably only the washing and a bit of cleanup for Sunday, besides caring for the children. Her mother would help, of course, but she couldn't do heavy work.

Devotions were late that morning. Rebecca smiled as she watched the children sing, their happy voices rising and falling as they sat on the couch and exuberantly trilled, "Peter, James, and John had a little sailboat . . ." She especially noted Dwightie, his face all alight with the joy of singing. How she loved him!

The morning passed quickly as Rebecca did laundry and kept a close eye on the children. Once, Dwight was found in the garden, dripping wet from a puddle of water, and another time he wandered off to visit Tía Woodsy's chickens. Rebecca did her best to convince him to stay in his favorite little spot in the yard where she could watch him. He called the spot his "pretty grass" because it was green and soft and lush there.

When Rebecca went to help Charlene and Karla to the bathroom, Judy asked about Dwight, and Rebecca told her where he was playing outside. When she came back, she heard Judy calling outside in a worried voice, "Dwight, Dwight! Where are you?"

"Girlies, do you know where Dwightie is?" Rebecca asked. It seemed strange that her mother should sound so panicked about him. Alarm seized her, and she joined the search. He wasn't in his pretty grass or down by the chickens where he had wandered off before.

Looking and calling, she asked her mother, "Did you check if he was with the sheep?" Judy had, and he wasn't there. As they continued to look and call with no success, Rebecca began to panic. Where could he have gone in such a short time?

They had already checked the dock, but they decided to go back there again. The water appeared calm under the lily pads, and nothing was to be seen. "Why don't you jump in and search for him?" Judy asked in a frightened voice.

Brian, the hired hand, was headed for the barn, but he joined in the search when Rebecca called to him, "Was this bucket lid here before?" It floated stark white on the surface of the pond.

"No!" he shouted back.

With a board she had picked up, Rebecca probed the water. The end of her board touched something hard and round, and as the lily pads drifted apart, suddenly a little body floated to the surface. Glimpsing just a part of him, Rebecca exclaimed, "Here he is!" Then with a heart-rending scream, she turned and yelled to Brian to come.

Those eternal moments of agony would be etched forever in her mind. The sound of Brian's boots thundering over the dock boards and the great splash as he dove into the water. The voice that sounded like some other than her own commanding him to give the child to her, the desperate moments that followed as she hugged Dwightie's soaked body to her and took him to dry land and laid him in the grass.

Rebecca and Brian worked over him. Someone called the ambulance. People began to arrive. For Rebecca, time stood still. Something deep within her seemed to whisper, "Let him go, let him go." But she couldn't. Not yet. Not till she had done all she could for him. When Curtis, their minister, and his daughter got there, they took over doing CPR till the medics arrived.

As the moments ticked by, Charlene and Karla came to sit in Rebecca's lap. "Dwightie fell in the water and got an ouchie," Rebecca explained with unnatural composure. "They are trying to help him get better. But if they can't help him, then he'll go to be with Jesus in heaven." The girls were solemn as they watched the fixed, staring eyes of their little play-mate who lay so still.

Rebecca dropped her head in her hands and covered her eyes that ached with unshed tears. An unexpected memory flitted through the disjointed thoughts whirling in her mind, and she remembered how she had always thought it would be special to have a child in heaven. A strange sort of awe wrapped her soul in light for a few solitary moments at the thought. But she knew she didn't want her baby to die.

At last the ambulance arrived. Courteously the driver asked people to move back. Kneeling by the body, he checked Dwightie over. Then, looking up into Rebecca's face, he said softly, "The child has died."

In that moment Rebecca wanted to cry out, "How can it be?" but something held her back. The words that finally came were calm. Placing her hand gently on her little boy's chest, she said, "Goodbye, my love. I'll see you in heaven." No tears came. The shock was too deep.

Kenneth's wife Geraldina and the children came, along with their close friend Martha Joy. People were crying softly. Rebecca called Rosy to tell her. Rosy responded in disbelief. She was in the hospital with a dying child, but she could hardly believe their healthy little boy was dead! Dennis and Kenneth were on their way to pick up Esther, who was also at the hospi-tal, and she waited anxiously at the door to give them the terrible news.

When the police arrived at the scene of the accident, they asked ques-tions and then drew aside to consult together. When they came back to the group, one of the officers spoke to Rebecca. "He is in a better place now, and God Himself will care for him."

"Yes, it is better there," Rebecca responded raggedly.

"We also have children, and we know how much this hurts. But we are going to have to ask everyone to step back now so we can cover the body with a sheet," the officer explained calmly.

"Can I hold him one more time, sir?" Rebecca's voice was calm, but tinged with anguish.

"No, I'm sorry. We need to proceed," the officer said.

They covered his little body and surrounded the scene with yellow tape. Someone fetched several umbrellas to shade the body from the hot sun. Rebecca, knowing she could not be with him, got up and went into the house. There would be things to prepare now that he was gone. There would have to be a funeral.

Rebecca walked woodenly to her room and knelt down. "God, I thank you for your presence with us in this difficult time. We accept this if this is your will. Help us in what lies ahead." Her words were dim with shock, yet she was aware that God was still present. When she saw his four little pairs of shoes in the shoe rack, she knew with a bittersweet pang that he would never scuff his little sandaled feet again.

Several hours later when his little body had been placed in a white bag and removed from the scene to the back of a pickup to be taken to the morgue, it started to rain. Looking up at the sullen sky, Rebecca felt as if the angels were weeping with her for her little boy.

When they went to buy a coffin that evening, they chose a little white one. Charlene, who was only three, was struggling very much to understand death, and occasionally broke out in a snatch of song about Dwightie being with the angels. It was December 20, 2008.

The next several days were a blur. When the body was brought back on Monday to be dressed, Rebecca was shocked to see the results of the autopsy—huge, ugly stitches all up his tummy and neck. She ironed a little set of clothes and dressed him with the help of others. Little Charlene tried to put on his sock, but Karla couldn't handle the sight of death. She snuggled into Dennis's lap and waited for the ordeal to be over.

Rebecca longed to hold her little boy and cuddle him and speak to him. But time was short, and in the heat the body wouldn't keep well. They hurried to finish dressing him, wrapping him in a blanket and gently placing him back in the coffin. As all the family gathered around before he was taken back to the morgue until the funeral, Dennis stepped forward. "Let's pray."

Reverently he thanked God for the short time they had been allowed to have Dwight as their own. Dwight had loved his tall grandpa, and Dennis had been deeply fond of him as well.

The viewing was on Tuesday and the funeral on Wednesday. Those were hard, long days for the grieving family, but their church surrounded them with love and support. One bright spot was that Selena began to recover, which enabled Rosy to attend the funeral. On Wednesday morning a friend called and asked Rebecca if she had seen the sunrise. The sky was bright with orange light that tinged the clouds in fiery beauty. "It's like Dwight's day has ended on earth, and his sun has risen in heaven," her friend shared thoughtfully. They had said "good night" to his short day on earth, but an eternal morning had dawned for him beyond the portals of heaven.

Before they took the casket to the church for the funeral, Rebecca opened it one last time and kissed her beloved baby farewell. After the funeral, when the time came for the burial, a deep peace had settled over her. It seemed to carry her somewhere above the anguish of her soul.

As they sang the words of one of Dwight's favorite songs, little Charlene sang heartily above the voices of the others from her perch in her Tío Kenneth's arms. Karla joined in more quietly from Dennis's.

Rebecca stood at the head of the grave and watched as dirt was gently sprinkled over the casket till the last bit of its tiny lid was covered. It was a moment of closure. Peace continued to carry her. When the grave was filled in entirely, Rebecca turned away and went out at the gate of the cemetery. Brian, who had retrieved Dwight's body from the pond, stood quietly by the gate with tears in his eyes. With a calm that only God could give, Rebecca looked at him and softly said, "Blessed be God."

The next evening at dusk Dennis and Judy accompanied Rebecca to the little freshly dug grave. As Rebecca knelt by it in the fading light, tears came as they would many times in the coming weeks and months. Tears of goodbye and tears of grief—her sweet baby was in heaven now forever, and someday she would meet him there. But the healing journey ahead looked long and painfully hard. As Rebecca rose to her feet, however, and walked away from the little mound of earth, she purposed in her heart to offer up her sorrow to God in trusting worship.

11

Jenny and Joselyn

In July 2009, over seven months after Dwightie died, Jenny joined the family. The two-year-old needed love desperately. Her black hair had turned yellow from lack of nutrition, and brain tuberculosis had left her entire left side paralyzed, including her face. Only her right hand could she move freely.

When the day came to pick Jenny up from the hospital, Judy and Dennis were gone on a lengthy trip to the States. Rebecca stayed home with the children while Rosy and Kenneth went to pick up Jenny. As Rosy and her oldest brother sped along the highway toward San José, she thought ahead to the little girl, lying lonely and waiting for someone to take her home. "It's time to have another baby in the house," she said to Kenneth, using the term they all used to describe their handicapped little ones. He nodded with a smile.

After six long hours of travel, they reached San José long after nightfall. By the time they found a parking lot and settled in to sleep in the van for the night, it was nearly midnight. As she went to sleep, Rosy whispered a prayer for the little girl she had never seen but already loved. "Oh, Father, you see this little girlie and all that she has already lived through. You know everything about her. If it is in your will, bring her home to us safely and soon. And show us how to care for and love her well."

"The morning sun and a hot cup of coffee sure are better than a hard van seat for a bed." Rosy stretched her sore muscles as she sipped her coffee the next morning.

Kenneth grimaced as he rubbed his back. "I'm just glad we made it here safely."

When they arrived at the hospital, they began the lengthy release process—paperwork, training on care and medications, and lots of waiting. Jenny was still on a treatment plan for her tuberculosis. She also had a feeding tube. As Rosy held her, she noted that her little head had been shaved of its sickly yellow hair for the shunt operation the doctors had had to perform twice, once to put it in and again to move it when it became infected.

At last the release process was finished, and as they drove through the busy city streets and out onto the highway along the coast, Rosy cuddled the child close. "Oh, darling Jenny. You're ours to love now, honey." Within four days of coming home, Jenny was eating by mouth. She ate and ate as if to make up for all the nutrients she had missed during her ravaging illness. One thing nagged at the girls, as Rosy remarked to Rebecca one day, "Have you noticed that Jenny almost never smiles?" Always her dark eyes were somber, her face watchful and sad. "We'll love you back to life again, little Jenny. Don't worry. Someday you'll smile again." Rosy rocked the little girl to sleep, hugging her close. Jenny rested peacefully against her.

Two weeks later in church, the breakthrough came. Esther and Rosy were singing with Jenny between them on the bench when they both heard it. Looking down, they realized that Jenny was trying to sing! Exchanging surprised glances, they grinned with delight. Little Jenny was singing! Rosy's heart warmed with praise as she thanked God for this major step in the healing progress.

From then on Jenny blossomed into new life. She learned to eat so well that they took her feeding tube out. She learned to balance herself and soon began to scoot around on the floor and play with toys and even get into mischief. "She's like a teething puppy," Rebecca exclaimed to Rosy, holding up a toy that had been gnawed full of teeth marks. And she had a special attraction for the trashcans, finding them whenever her caregiver's back was turned even for a few moments.

One day Rosy noticed with alarm that Jenny was having a mild convulsion. Calling the pediatrician, she asked what she should do. "Take her to the emergency room immediately. I'll meet you there," he said. In the emergency room they confirmed that Jenny was having seizures. After injecting her with a seizure medication, they put in a PICC[1] line for ease of treatment. She was admitted overnight.

"You don't like that tube, do you, Jenny darling?" Rosy could tell her little girl was restless and wanted to pull the tube out. "Here, let's put a sock on your hand. You have to leave it in." Jenny seemed to give up pulling at the tube, and after feeding her, Rosy could tell she was sleepy. Singing to her softly, Rosy soon had Jenny sleeping and laid her in her crib.

In the middle of the night Rosy went to check on her. Startled, she noticed that the PICC line wasn't where it belonged. Jenny had it in her mouth! It appeared she had pulled it out with her teeth.

Going over to the window of the nurse's station, Rosy tapped on the glass, and the nurse came to check. "We'll have to wake her up and put it back in," the nurse said ruefully. Jenny was disconcerted by this state of affairs, but it had to be done. Both Rosy and Jenny were glad to go home the following day.

---

[1] PICC: Peripherally inserted central catheter

Jenny's father came to visit her a few times while she was with the Kropfs. "It seems odd to me that Jenny's father comes at all to see the girlie," Rosy said after one of his visits. "He hardly holds her and he always seems so stiff."

"I've noticed that too," Esther exclaimed. "And his questions are almost always about our other foster children and not about his own daughter's development." The Kropfs were aware that Jenny's parents were fighting in the welfare system for parental rights, and they knew the time might come when they would have to give her up. The lack of affection Jenny's father showed and her family's desperately poor living conditions made the sisters reluctant to see the little girl return to her family.

"I hope this sweet little girl won't go back to her family, at least not for a while," Rosy fretted to Rebecca.

In the heat of the same July that Jenny came to live with them, a call came for another little girl. Six-month-old Joselyn had been born with severe brain damage as the result of a disease her mother had contracted from cats. Her thirteen-year-old mother had been turned out on the street by her family, and with nowhere to live with her baby who had a number of special health needs, the young mother had to leave her in the hospital. Although she was a devoted little mother who loved her baby deeply, she had no alternative in her present situation.

Now, with swine flu ravaging the hospital, the welfare department wanted to remove her to a safe home environment. "See if you can find another place for her. If you can't, then call us back," Dennis told them, knowing that having Jenny was going to fill their time.

Two days after the first phone call about Joselyn, a second call came, and the Kropfs agreed to take her for the weekend. The hospital could find no other short-term placement. By suppertime that evening she had arrived, and they were holding a beautiful little girl in their arms.

With her fine features and silky black hair, Joselyn looked like a baby doll. Her chubby cherubic cheeks told that she was well fed. But she was quite dirty. A bath was one of the first orders of the evening. When Joselyn was all bundled in clean clothes and a light blanket, Rosy sat down in the rocking chair and sang to her.

Joselyn's little arms were stiff, and her whole body was tight from tension. Rosy began to plan therapy to help her gain relief. Her heart already overflowed with ideas and plans for helping this baby girl. There were so many things she wanted to do for her!

Saturday passed, and all the girls and Judy enjoyed taking turns holding Joselyn. It was special having a tiny baby in the house again. She was primarily Rosy's charge, though.

On Sunday Rosy didn't take the baby to church. Fragile little Joselyn needed time to adjust. That night Joselyn wouldn't go to sleep. For a long time Rosy held her, talking to her and stroking her soft hair, rocking her and singing to her. But she refused to be lulled to slumber. The hours crept on, and as the evening grew very late, Rosy finally laid the wakeful but quiet baby in her crib.

When she checked her in the middle of the night, she was still awake. It seemed odd, but she seemed peaceful, so Rosy fed her and went back to bed. In the morning Rosy could tell something wasn't quite right. She hadn't had Joselyn long enough to know what her normal self was like, but she could tell the baby had hardly slept all night, and she seemed sick.

"I think we probably should just take her to the emergency room and make sure everything is okay," Dennis said after they had talked it over. Rosy left her in Judy's arms while she went to get a few things ready to go to the hospital.

When she came back through the living room where Judy was cuddling the baby, she saw immediately that something was wrong. Judy's face was wet with tears, and baby Joselyn was gasping for breath despite her oxygen tube. *She sounds as though she is dying!* Rosy thought in panic. She rushed over and bent down to look into Joselyn's pale little face. She took her briefly in her arms to see if there was anything she could do to help.

"Hurry, Rosy, you need to get her to the hospital!" Tears choked her mother's voice.

Handing her back to Judy, Rosy rushed to throw their things in the van and then came back for the baby. Dennis gunned the engine to life and tore out the lane as fast as he dared to drive over the rough spots and potholes.

When they reached the last long hill before the main road, the van got stuck in a mud hole caused by a heavy rain the night before. "You'll have to get out and push, Rosy," Dennis instructed hurriedly.

Laying the baby down, Rosy hopped out and rushed to the back of the van, unmindful of the splattering mud. She pushed with all her strength, and the van plunged and spun until it reached solid ground again. Huffing, Rosy clambered back into the van, wiped the mud from her hands, and picked up the baby again.

Her heart beat hard as she held Joselyn gently and prayed desperately for God's mercy. Halfway into town she looked at the still face and somehow knew. "Daddy, I think it's too late. I think she's already gone."

When they got to the emergency room, the head doctor put his stethoscope on her chest. He quietly shook his head. "Gone."

The team who had gathered to go into action when she arrived drifted away, and Rosy sat quietly beside the little body. A silent ache throbbed somewhere deep inside her, overshadowed by a painful sense of failure.

A little later a nurse came in and asked gently, "Shall we remove the tubes? She won't need them now." Rosy wiped a silent tear and nodded jerkily. When the nurse had gone again, Rosy marveled at how pretty Joselyn looked. Without tubes, her natural sweetness and beauty was even more evident. And the pain lines had vanished from her face too. She looked like a baby in a perfectly blissful sleep.

Soon they moved the tiny body to another room where Rosy sat for a short time, waiting, praying, pondering. She looked up when a male nurse entered. "We'll need to take the body now," he said. Rosy watched mournfully as he wrapped the wee baby girl in a sheet and covered her face, taping the bundle shut and writing her name on the tape. Then he left for the morgue, and Rosy was left alone.

Before they left the hospital, she stopped to see the pediatrician who had been caring for Joselyn in the hospital. Through teary eyes and with a lump in her throat, she looked at the kind doctor and asked, "What did I do wrong?"

"You did nothing wrong," the doctor said gently. "Nothing at all. It was her time to go."

Later a nurse told them she thought the baby, whose death was caused by the brain damage with which she had been born, had waited till she was in a peaceful place to die. "Children like this often do that," she said, referring to children who are terminal and who lack someone to nurture them. Later Rebecca and Rosy would wonder if the absence of her birth mother had taken the baby's will to live.

They would need to let the family bury the baby. But they bought a little white coffin and took the body home for a funeral service. They asked the bishop's daughter, Lucille, to make a little white dress for her which they picked up on the way home.

Back home they gently bathed and dressed the tiny body. Shedding quiet tears, they prepared her for the 3:00 service that afternoon. It was the only time she would ever go to church with them in the three days she had been part of their little family. The taxi the hospital had sent to retrieve her body arrived before they had even left for the church. They told the taxi driver it would be a short service, and he agreed to sit in on the service and wait for them. He followed the van to the church house on the hill.

Before the service all the little children gathered around, touching

Joselyn's small hands gently and looking solemnly into her sweet face. The tiny casket was set in front of the pulpit. They sang a bit, Kenneth read the simple obituary, and Brother Herman, their bishop, gave a short devotional. Then they closed the casket, and the taxi driver reverently took the body from them.

As the taxi drove away with that tiny casket in the back, Rosy watched with silent tears coursing down her face. She had loved Joselyn for such a short time, and the grief was different from what it had been for Dwightie. But it was still grief nonetheless.

Another loss followed shortly on its heels. The welfare office in the district where Jenny's family lived seemed convinced that the father had a great deal of affection for, and a strong interest in, his daughter. Jenny had become a sparkling, happy child in her eight months with the Kropfs, and was even learning to walk a little when the news came that the social workers were transferring her to another foster home close to her birth family. It was a hard blow for all of them, but especially for Rosy.

The Kropfs were relieved to find out that the new foster parents for Jenny were a kind, childless couple who would take superb care of her. But it still hurt tremendously to let her go. Whenever she came back for visits, she always seemed to remember her first foster home, especially the locations of the toy box and trashcans. They couldn't have loved one of their own children more. Jenny continued in their prayers and hearts long after she had passed out of their arms into those of others.

One afternoon as the sisters sipped coffee together, they reflected on their recent losses.

"There was so much I wanted to do for Joselyn," Rosy told Rebecca. "And so little I felt I could do. Three days. That's not enough time."

"Rosy, He sees the sparrow fall. She's safe with Him now." Rebecca put her arm around Rosy's shoulder. "You loved her so well. Her life and death are in His hands."

"I know, and I'm at peace to leave her there. But the grief is real."

"I know. I understand. Death is so painful. We've experienced so many losses; our brother Leonard when we were small children, then Dwight, and now Joselyn. Even Jenny leaving for another foster home was a loss we had to grieve. And Marco—it hurts so much to see him reject everything we tried to teach him about God's love for him. Sometimes my heart wants to burst with pain. Then I remember what a gift each of them has been to us. Looking back, I wouldn't trade one day I had with little Dwightie. I'm thankful for every one of them. Rosy, someday we'll go be with our little angels."

"Someday," Rosy nodded wistfully. "Some days I ache to go Home right away."

"Me too. Come quickly, Lord Jesus," Rebecca agreed fervently. The words that poured from their bruised hearts formed a song of faith in God's ultimate goodness. Out of their pain and loss, another verse in a doxology of praise rose up to their Lord.

12

Baby Joe

I t was the beginning of dry season, the time of year when tourists flock to San José for vacation to enjoy the balmy temperatures and consistently sunny days. But it wasn't vacation that brought Rosy to San José that week in January 2012. Selena had been admitted to the children's hospital for yet another surgery. This tan, stucco hospital with its four stories of verandas, flat orange roof, and palm-lined drive was now well known by all three of the girls due to their children's frequent visits there.

That week Rebecca took yet another call from the welfare department. "We have a preemie baby boy who needs a placement. His name is Joe. He's in the children's hospital in San José," the social worker told her.

"Rosy, I think this might excite you," Rebecca told her sister after informing her parents. "The next baby is yours, you know." Rebecca watched Rosy's eyes light up. Her arms had felt strangely empty in the two-and-a-half years since Joselyn's death, even though she had plenty to do. "You should go see him."

So Rosy met with the social worker handling Joe's case and asked if she could see the baby.

"Follow me," the social worker said, beckoning with her hand. For the first time in her life, Rosy found herself in the neonatal unit of the hospital.

It's like a world made up of smaller worlds, Rosy thought. Each incubator contained a tiny atmosphere all its own with controlled temperature, oxygen, and lighting, and was attended by specialized doctors and nurses. Inside these private bubbles lay tiny babies fighting for life. Joe had been one of these babies.

Now, at two months old, he weighed six pounds and had graduated to a crib. His dark eyes were sleepy, and his lovely brown skin was baby soft. "Would you like to feed him?" the nurse asked. Rosy didn't hesitate. As she held that little bundle in her arms, something happened in her heart. She fell in love with this little baby boy. He blinked up at her and sucked listlessly on his bottle.

"Why won't he take his milk?" she asked the nurse after several moments.

Coming to stand beside her, the nurse looked at the bottle and shrugged. "He's used to being fed in his bed. He probably won't drink because you're holding him."

She could only hold him for fifteen short minutes before he had to go back in his crib. "You are so precious and tiny," Rosy murmured as she cradled him in her arms. She would have taken him home that day if she had been allowed. But the head nurse would be coming soon, and she didn't want to get scolded for being in the neonatal unit, even though she had official permission. "I'll come for you later, Baby Joe," she whispered. She gently gave him back to the nurse and reluctantly followed the social worker out into the long, echoing corridor.

When she wasn't in the hospital, Rosy was caring for her Charlene and Selena in her little house across the banana patch from her family's residence. When the family had consulted the ministry about taking on another baby, they concluded that Rosy should have Joe in her house so it would be less noise and stress for Judy, whose health was fragile. Her heart was giving her more trouble these days.

So it was that after being scrubbed and rearranged to accommodate a crib, the house was ready for its newest occupant. Joe came home with oxygen and rather grim prospects. He'd had meningitis, and the doctors said he had severe brain damage. He also had a cyst on his brain and a mild heart condition. But he looked entirely normal. The six-and-a-quarter-pound bundle of love was welcomed with open arms and hearts as he made his debut in the family.

His weight gain took off now, and he grew by leaps and bounds. Soon he was able to be weaned off oxygen as well. As she watched him grow day by day, Rosy's heart almost burst with love for the little fellow. He was simply adorable with his sweet round face and big dark eyes that cheerfully took in all of life around him. Watching a baby develop and grow from such a tiny age through all the minute stages was a joy for her, and every day with him was a treasure.

Then she noticed that his head seemed to be growing rather quickly. She supposed that a baby's head did grow, but Joe's seemed to be growing faster than normal. Rosy took him to the doctor, who confirmed her fears. His head was growing because of fluid buildup. He would have to be admitted to the hospital immediately.

It was a Friday, and there would be no room in the operating schedule for him until Monday, but they performed an ultrasound right away. After confirming that fluid buildup was taking place, they inserted a large needle into his head to drain off fluid and relieve some of the pressure until the surgery could be performed.

Rosy noticed his nearly immediate relief. As she fed him his bottle that night, he seemed calmer and more relaxed. "That pressure on your head has been hurting you, hasn't it, poor baby?" She cuddled him a lot over the weekend. Then on Monday she told him goodbye and sent him into surgery.

He came back from surgery and recovery howling with hunger. He bounced back quickly, and within a day he was ready to go home. How thankful and relieved Rosy was when she was settled once more at home with her foster son doing well!

"Look at his eyes sparkle," Rebecca said one day. "He's just like a magnet! Everyone who sees him wants to hold him."

"I know, isn't he just adorable?" Esther patted his head. The two foster *tías* were enjoying the plump four-month-old baby of the family almost as much as Rosy was.

"He seems to be developing almost normally for a preemie of his age," Rebecca said.

"I was thinking the same thing." Rosy beamed at the little man. "He seems almost normal to me. All this stuff about severe brain damage doesn't seem very accurate. I think he's going to be much closer to normal than they've predicted."

"But either way, all our babies are precious." Esther glanced around the room at the other children, who were playing happily. She knew they all felt the same about each of their babies being equally special. But sometimes it was hard for her to know that her special charges, Andy and Kimberly, would never be able to respond fully to her love. They could smile, though, and she knew they felt the love they received. She longed for them to express themselves like other children, but knew in her aching heart that it wouldn't happen until the day when their beautiful souls would be released from their limited bodies and be free in heaven with Jesus. "Someday, all our babies will be free of every limitation. Won't that be amazing?" she asked passionately.

Rebecca and Rosy both agreed heartily.

"You know, sometimes I ponder the days when we started working with the children, and I think about who the work is really for." Rebecca stroked Karla's dark hair as the little girl rested in her lap. "We don't have to worry about the souls of most of our children since they don't have the power to make the choice. It's like the soul of a baby. But I can't help realizing that we are impacting souls for the kingdom of God. I don't think the work is for the children; I think it's for their families and the people we meet in the hospital."

"Like Anabel." Esther held Andy close and rocked him as she spoke, remembering a young woman they had met in one of their stays at the hospital. "When her special-needs son died, it was an open door for us to be there for her. Now we have a strong friendship, and we are able to speak into her life."

"And like the time we saw Kimberly and Selena's mom in the hospital when she was there with their little sister," Rosy said.

"She was so heartbroken about her girls and seemed to feel so guilty for leaving them. It was a gift to be able to care for her in her sorrow and let her know that her little girls are being loved and taken care of in a Christian home," Esther remembered.

"I can't help thinking of Gerald's family too," Rebecca said. "It's been such a gift to have them all visit us here and so special to get to have his sisters stay here."

"I love how his siblings just soak up truth like little sponges." Esther tossed a bouncy ball to Charlene. "They aren't here more than an hour before they ask for a songbook and start to sing."

"And Bible stories. They asked me to read more and more the last time they were here. I just pray that someday their little hearts will make a long-term decision to follow Jesus and the truth they seem so eager to drink up." Rebecca sighed. "I wish I could do more for them. Sometimes I feel so limited, but I guess every opportunity is a gift, and every seed planted is a chance for the truth to grow."

"People seem so hungry for truth nowadays. Remember when Daddy spoke to that group of kindergarten teachers at the children's hospital?"

"Yeah, weren't there around eighty teachers in attendance?"

"And they asked him to speak for fifteen minutes. He chose to speak on where truth is found and how the Bible is the truth. He said that when he gave out tracts on the authority of Scripture, they just devoured them. With the interest they showed, it makes me wonder how many of them have made decisions toward God."

"We'll have to keep praying for all these situations." Esther rose to give seven-year-old Andy his shower. "With eternity ahead, every moment of investment counts, but the seeds can only grow as His Holy Spirit does the work in their hearts."

Rosy gave baby Joe a kiss on his fuzzy head and hugged him close. He cuddled against her and looked up with dark, questioning eyes. Then a smile spread across his now chubby face. "Every moment counts, Joe. I pray someday you'll be a God-fearing man. Your soul is priceless, little darling."

13

Little Brown Leaf

"Thou art my servant; I have chosen thee, and not cast thee away." Rebecca listened as her father's deep voice read the familiar passage reverently. "Fear thou not; for I am with thee: be not dismayed; for I am thy God: I will strengthen thee; yea, I will help thee; yea, I will uphold thee with the right hand of my righteousness."[1]

Rebecca noticed that her mother seemed to be especially drinking in the words today. When they had started reading through Isaiah for family devotions recently, Judy had commented on how much the book had meant to her and how many beautiful passages in it were special to her as well. She had been weak and fighting an infection for over a week, and the words of strength and courage soothed her soul.

After rising from their knees after Dennis prayed, the girls started discussing their plans for the day. Esther and Rosy were planning to go mango picking along with their sister-in-law Geraldina. Several of the nephews would join them after school. They were taking a lunch along,

---

[1] Isaiah 41:9–10

and Rosy planned to take little Joe in the baby carrier. But the sky promised a rain storm shortly, and Rosy was rethinking her original plan.

"Do you want me to come along instead?" Rebecca offered spontaneously. The girls agreed they could use the extra help, and after donning boots, the crew of fruit pickers set off. Judy said goodbye from the porch. As Rebecca turned and said, "Goodbye, Mama," she felt a strange nudge inside her soul, but without another thought about it, she went on her way. The rain started shortly, but the merry band of pickers headed bravely down the valley to collect their treasure.

Judy sat and rested in her chair most of the morning. She was too sick to help Rosy bring in wash or make dinner. She had often been sick over her nineteen years as a cardiac patient, but now she seemed worse than ever. Soon she went to lie down. Rosy had her hands full with baby Joe and the other six children, along with Geraldina's little Susan and Ezra, who had cut his foot and needed to lay low for a time. However, everyone cooperated, and the morning passed rather uneventfully.

At lunch Rosy noticed that Judy seemed shaky when she brought her plate to the table. After taking only a bite or two of food, she said, "I can't. I'll just go lie down."

"Mama, are you okay?" Rosy, concerned, paused in dishing up Ezra's plate.

"I'm just getting a fever again," she said weakly and went to lie down.

That afternoon Selena seemed to be running a fever. Rosy had just gotten home from the hospital with her on Saturday after her tonsils had been removed, and now the little girl tossed and turned, miserable from the pain and swelling. Rosy worried that the fever might mean that infection had set in. But she couldn't seem to find the thermometer to check for sure.

When the children had finished their lunch, Rosy sent them to take naps. Finally all of them were tucked in, and Rosy, exhausted from a busy morning, picked up baby Joe and settled into the recliner with a bottle.

As she fed him and rocked him, she watched his dark eyes slowly close. When he was asleep, she just sat and read and rocked, resting.

Suddenly there was a sickening *thud* in the hall. Rosy started up in alarm. *What was that sound?* she wondered, listening. She got up and looked down the hall. There lay her mother, collapsed on the floor!

Plopping baby Joe onto the couch, where he immediately woke and started to cry, Rosy rushed to Judy's side. "Mama!" she cried worriedly. "Mama! Are you okay? Daddy! Come quick! Mama fell!"

Dennis rushed into the room from another part of the house. Rosy had dialed Kenneth's number by that time and told him, "Come quick!" and hung up. He came over immediately.

Judy was hardly breathing, and her face had turned purple. They could feel no pulse. A big gasp was followed by several more, twenty seconds apart.

"Oxygen!" exclaimed Rosy.

"Yes, get it!" Dennis said distractedly.

Rushing to Judy's side with the small oxygen tank they kept for Andy's use, they turned it on. She responded right away. She began to breathe again, and as her heart started beating once more, blood gushed from a wound on the back of her head. She breathed in deep groans, but remained unconscious.

Rosy called the ambulance, and the children had soon gathered around where Grandma lay hurt. Charlene held a crying baby Joe, and Ezra held his little sister Susan, who cried and screamed in fear. Karla came over too, and Rosy asked Kenneth to take her, since she would panic from the trauma and the other children crying. He picked her up gently and set her in the living room on the recliner.

"There's so much blood." Dennis's voice held desperation as he tried to hold the wound shut with pressure, using cloth after cloth to sop up the sticky, red flow.

Meanwhile the mango pickers had been told that Judy was dying, and they dropped their buckets and ran. Julian, a brother from their church, picked them up in his van and got them home before the ambulance arrived.

The girls rushed into the house, not knowing what they would find. Two-year-old Ezra sat crying in Judy's chair while Kenneth tried to soothe his hysterical baby daughter. Dennis sat at the table, ready to go with the ambulance when it arrived. He was talking on the phone with Judy's doctor.

Judy seemed to drift in and out of consciousness now. It was when she heard Esther's brisk voice that she roused a bit. She gave each of them what seemed to be a look of recognition, and she gave Dennis a beautiful smile.

As soon as the ambulance team had come and gone, time stood still. Dennis called from the hospital after several hours to tell them that the doctors didn't think it was a heart attack. "They think it was syncope—that she passed out because there wasn't enough blood flow to the brain. They are trying to stabilize her right now, and she will be kept in obser- vation overnight."

With morning came more bad news. The nurses had given permission for her to get up and use the restroom in the middle of the night. When they unhooked the oxygen and Dennis tried to help her get up, she sat up and said, "I can't," before falling back onto the pillow. She went into cardiac arrest, and they had to shock her heart to get it beating again. The family's spirits sank when they heard this, and Kenneth and the girls wanted to see their mother before things got any worse.

An ambulance transferred her to another hospital in San José that morning, so the whole family went up to the main road to meet it as it went by. When it came into sight, its sirens blaring, Rebecca's heart jumped. Dennis opened the door and thrust out several things for them to take home in exchange for the food and clothing they had gathered for him. They caught only a glimpse of their beloved mother. But even so, it was almost more than they could bear. Her whole body heaved with the effort of breathing. She was attached to all kinds of equipment and tubes.

How heart-rending to watch the conveyance go flashing and screaming on its way, not knowing if they would ever see their mother alive again!

Back home, Rosy worried about Selena, who was dehydrated and burning with fever. "Please, can we pray for her?" If things didn't change shortly, they would have to take her to the hospital also. They gathered around with some others who had come to be there, including Aunt Mary, the wife of Mama's youngest uncle. Aunt Mary put her hand tenderly on Selena and prayed simply for God's healing touch and protective care for her during this time of crisis.

The ministry met with Kenneth and the girls in the bakery to discuss how to proceed. Dennis wanted their input even though he wasn't there. Judy had been through at least eleven surgeries. If the doctors recommended it, should she undergo yet another operation? The ministers advised that even if it didn't look likely that Judy would recover without surgery, the family should respect Judy's wish not to have heart surgery again.

When they came in from the bakery, Selena's fever had broken. They found relief in this gentle reminder that God was still caring for them and would watch over the unfolding details of the coming hours and days.

Rebecca had gotten ready to go to the hospital to take a turn at Judy's bedside so Dennis could get a bit of rest. Dennis called and said that he had been out briefly with Uncle Richard and Aunt Ellen, and when he had come back in, Judy had gone into cardiac arrest again. This time they had needed to shock her heart twice to get it beating again. She wasn't in condition for surgery.

When Rebecca got to the hospital and saw her father, he looked haggard. "I wish you could have a chance to rest." She laid her hand on his arm. "You look like you need it."

Rebecca entered Judy's room with trepidation. When she saw her beloved mother, her heart cried out in pain. She was hooked to a ventilator with tubes in her mouth and a mask over part of her face. Tubes were everywhere.

Weary from the past two days of exertion, Rebecca sank into the chair at the bedside, in dire need of rest herself. But her mother needed her more. Through the long watches of the evening and into the night, she bathed Judy's forehead and held her swollen hand and rubbed her arms. The steady *bleep, bleep* of the monitors and the other whispering night sounds of the hospital blended into sad shadows as Rebecca mourned at seeing her mother so helpless.

She knew how much Judy wished to go to heaven and leave her weary, pain-racked body behind. But Rebecca couldn't help wishing and longing for healing. Life would never be the same if their mother were to leave them. Silently she prayed. Softly she quoted Psalm 23:4 again and again: "Yea, though I walk through the valley of the shadow of death, I will fear no evil: for thou art with me." In the wee hours of the morning, she went to the chapel for a few winks of sleep. She was utterly exhausted.

When the doctor made rounds, she kindly took time for all of Rebecca's questions. She confirmed that the extremely dilated pupils indicated brain damage and that visiting time would be cut down considerably if she were moved to the intensive care unit.

"We don't want more intensive measures taken, and if her heart stops again, my father asked that she not be shocked anymore," Rebecca told the doctor, her voice strained but resolute. She did not want to go home that day, but knew she would have to take her turn with the children. "This may be my last chance to be with Mama," she murmured to herself.

Then Rebecca received word that young women from the church would babysit the children that day. Fighting tears of relief and thankfulness, she stayed at the hospital until her sisters and Kenneth came that evening. When they arrived, the siblings decided that Esther would stay for the night, but that the rest of them would go after spending the evening with their mother.

As soon as Esther walked into the room, she began to talk to Judy and fix her clothes and bedding to make her as comfortable as possible. She had the touch of a nurse with bedridden people, and she knew exactly how to make them most comfortable. When she bent down and whispered, "Mama, I'm Esther and I'm going to stay with you for the night," Judy opened her eyes and looked at her.

Esther talked to her, rubbed her feet and hands, and quoted Psalm 23 to her just as Rebecca had done the night before. Esther took extra care to clean out her mouth and clean her cut, which had begun to look infected. She arranged her comfortably, thinking, *The nurses don't know what position is best for her.* She tried to sleep in a hard-backed chair with her head on the edge of the bed.

More than once during that long night, Judy's ventilator screeched its warning and her airway had to be suctioned out. Her lips and hands and face were purple from lack of air. When Esther saw that, she started to cry.

"Go hug her." The nurse nudged Esther toward her mother. Esther bent down and embraced her frail loved one. Then she straightened and called her father to come. He had been resting in another part of the hospital. Soon he took his place at Judy's side. It seemed Judy was able to rest peacefully for only brief periods after the clogged ventilator tube was suctioned.

Later that morning as Rosy and Kenneth drove to the hospital to see Judy, Rosy received a call from social services in San Marco where baby Joe's parents lived. "We'll be coming on Tuesday to pick Joe up and return him to his birth parents. We will be there at 9:00. Have his things ready so you don't delay us," came the sterile instruction.

"I didn't know anything about this." Rosy clenched the phone in agitation.

"Well, I would have thought the welfare department there would have informed you," the woman said.

When Rosy called the local welfare department to inquire, the social worker there was shocked and said she didn't realize the social services department had decided to return him. Their case lawyer checked into it, though, and confirmed that it was true. Rosy felt like the world was spinning out of control. She didn't have the capacity to process the shock in the midst of such a major crisis. She told her father about it, but they were careful not to let Judy hear. How it would have broken her heart to know they were losing Joe!

By now Judy was burning with fever. Rebecca prayed that her brother Michael would make it in time. He and his wife Jessica were flying in from the States and coming straight to the hospital. They wanted to have time to say goodbye.

The rest of the family, gathered around Judy's bedside, could see death's pallor slowly creeping into her face. Yet she seemed to be holding on for her youngest son.

The following day, three days after Judy was hospitalized, Michael and his wife Jessica arrived. When Jessica walked in, she kissed the dear face and exclaimed gently, "Oh, Mom, you don't have to stay for us." The vigil continued. As they watched her suffer, the family had started to pray, "Lord, please take her soon."

All was dark and long and silent, and the hours seemed to blur together. Sometime in the night Rebecca looked into her mother's face with tenderness. "Mama, dear." Her voice was soft and teary. "You are so tired, Mama. If the angels come for you, and if you want to go with them, just go. They will help you to cross the Jordan River, and God will take care of us. We'll be all right. You can just go so you won't hurt anymore." The family's familiar doxology of faith and praise was again emerging from a heart of anguish. As Rebecca continued to gaze into her face, Judy gave a short gasp, and then another. Rebecca's heart pounded as she wondered if her mother was going right then, but she continued to breathe.

But from that point, her breaths started coming farther and farther apart. The lady in the next bed was passing into eternity at the same time.

The granddaughter of the woman came and asked to use Esther's phone. She was loud and abrasive, and it felt like an intrusion into a sacred place to have her abruptly yank back the curtain and ask for the phone, and then talk so loudly right beside them. But when they saw the old woman who had passed, they could feel nothing but pity for her and her family.

Earlier in the day, one of the nurses had looked at Judy's face and exclaimed, "She has so much peace." At that moment Rebecca had wondered how the woman could say such a thing when Judy was in agony. But now, as she observed this other elderly woman's face through a crack in the curtain, she noticed that the woman looked as if she had died in the grip of a demon. Even in death, anguish and horror contorted her face. The stark reality of an unprepared soul slipping into eternity brought pain to Rebecca's heart. How precious, in contrast, her mother's imminent passage home! Sometime during the day, Rebecca noticed a rainbow outside the hospital window—a promise of God's faithfulness in the midst of pain. He would not fail.

At 2:25 a.m. on June 15, 2012, as the family stood around her bed, Judy Kropf breathed her last and passed into glory. All her suffering was over forever. At last she would be face to face with the One she had loved and faithfully served.

The funeral was hard to plan; they were all so exhausted and numb. One of their ministers, Brother Marlin, preached the funeral message from verses Judy had marked in her Bible. Somewhere in the message, he read a poem called "Little Brown Leaf" that Judy had always loved. Her daughters knew that she had often identified with the words.

> A lone, shriveled leaf at the top of a tree
> Flutters in wind and snow.
> "Little brown leaf at the top of the tree,
> Why don't you just let go?

"Why don't you flutter down to the ground
And hide in the winter snow?
There the winds don't beat and the storms don't rage.
Why don't you just let go?

"Soft on the bosom of Mother Earth,
Quiet and sweet and slow,
Gently into the welcoming night,
Why don't you just let go?"

"I didn't place me here," said the leaf.
"I didn't choose to grow;
But there's One who did, and He alone
Will choose when I shall go.

"Until that day, I've a purpose here,
Not all of which I know;
But I'll smile at the storm and I'll sing in the gale
Till the Master lets me go!" [2]

And the Master had let her go! But those left behind felt the absence of her smile and song and the ache of the parting as they watched her casket being lowered into the dark earth, the rain pouring down on them. Dennis didn't seem to mind the rain, though. It ran in rivulets down his neck and dripped off the rim of his hat. *At the age of sixty-four, I've just said goodbye to my dearest earthly friend,* he thought.

The emptiness and ache seemed palpable as they drove back to the house that night. Even though the sisters were grown women in their thirties, they felt like lost children without their mother. *Things will never be the same,* Rebecca thought heavily. Those same thoughts reverberated through her soul on Tuesday when they said goodbye to baby Joe as well.

---

[2] Author unknown

"It feels almost like another funeral," Rosy sighed to Rebecca, wiping her eyes yet again.

"It does!" Rebecca said. "It all seems too hard. My heart is so weary. I just feel like I'm crying out every moment, but almost too weary to cry out to God for help."

"It's like there is just loss after loss." Rosy's eyes were dark with grief. "I just can't understand why they had to take Joe!"

"I'm so sorry." Rebecca reached out and put her arm around Rosy's shoulder. Silent tears slipped down their cheeks as they cried together.

"And I wouldn't wish Mama back in her suffering body, but I can't tell you how much I miss her already. The grief journey looks too hard." The sisters sat in silence for some moments, each wrapped in her own painful reflections as they would often do in the months of grieving to come.

A year later, on the anniversary of Judy's passing into glory, the family took a bouquet of flowers to her grave to celebrate and remember. "Mama so longed for her time of rest in heaven," Rebecca said. "I think I'm realizing that she got there one weary, painful day at a time. No matter what she faced, she always trusted God. We want to continue serving faithfully too, until that glorious day when there won't be any more goodbyes and we'll be with Jesus forever."

Esther nodded, wiping tears. "She loved so well. I want to live and love as well as she did." Rosy gave her a tight hug, and after several moments of silence, the family turned to go quietly out of the graveyard and back to living faithfully in the life He had given them, one day at a time, through losses and trials, until He called them home.

14

Threats

"Sometimes I feel fearful of what those boys will do next," Rebecca told Rosy in the kitchen one morning. "They are like a gang!"

"I'm afraid too, sometimes," Esther joined the conversation as she came into the room. "They are known in the church neighborhood as the hooligans after the incident with Herman's family."

Marco, the conflicted little boy who used to call Dennis "Daddy," had grown into a rebellious youth while living with his birth family for the last several years. Although his grandmother, Lola, still belonged to the Mennonite church, it seemed that her grandson and her son, José, were determined to reject whatever godly teaching they had heard. Several other boys, including a young man named Jorge, associated with them. José was the declared leader of the group and the only one over eighteen years of age. The trouble they caused had only been accelerating for the last several years.

One day they bombarded Bishop Herman Yoder's van with big balls of dried clay. One lump shattered the windshield. Thankfully no one was hurt. But the attack shook the bishop's family. "You need to talk to the parents about this," someone advised Herman. So Herman called Jorge's father and talked to José's mother about the trouble.

The next day Jorge's father came and made his son apologize. "We gladly forgive you," Herman said kindly. The teenager, abashed and frightened, left with a downcast face. But Herman felt satisfied that they had parted on good terms. José found out about the forced apology and never extended any remorse for his behavior.

With José and his family as next-door neighbors, just across the wall from their family, Herman and Linda found it a constant challenge to relate to the troubled young man and his gang. One Sunday afternoon they came home to find three knives driven into the wall and a large blade sticking out of the door of their shop. Frightened, they reported it to the police.

But things continued to grow worse. The troublemakers vandalized the church school, tearing up textbooks, strewing things around, and even urinating on some of the books.

"It's just going from bad to worse," Esther told Rebecca as they discussed the neighborhood gang once more. "The day they vandalized Herman and Linda's house really left the Yoders feeling shaken."

"I know. Linda told me about it," Rebecca said sadly. "They went into the master bedroom and dumped clothes and gifts and other items from the dresser all over the floor. They opened a large can of tuna and took a scoop out and cut into a cake and scattered it all over the floor."

"How rude!" Esther shuddered indignantly. "I didn't hear all the details."

"Then they took a large bag, filled it with small items such as binoculars, and made their escape. Before leaving, they painted big letters on the wall that read, 'Tornado, thanks a lot. We love ya.' "

Their crude, mysterious sarcasm, coupled with their vicious acts of destruction, left the family feeling deeply violated. What had gotten into these boys, and what were they trying to communicate?

The gang created two holes in the dense underbrush lining the road. They would crawl in and lie in wait for the college-age girls of the community to pass, then jump out and scare them. Once they accosted a man on horseback and would not let him go until someone came to help him. The gang threatened to kill anyone who reported their behavior.

Their viciousness accelerated rapidly. People suspected drug activity. The gang started butchering people's cows and pigs at random. They invaded the Kropf home and Rosy's little house in the banana patch as well as Kenneth's big house. They found Geraldina's journal and left it open to a page where she had written about the vandalism taking place in the neighborhood. She had written, "We think we know who it is . . ." but she was grateful that she had not written the names of those whom they suspected. The larger community of neighbors suffered at their hands as well. One man declared that if the gang stepped on his farm, they would be dead men. The Mennonite community prayed desperately for deliverance. Then the rumor came that the gang had been hired for the coffee harvest in another area. How relieved the community felt to hear that the vandals had left the area! "I think God answered our prayers," Linda told Herman with a sigh. "I was about done in with all the things they've been doing lately. I didn't know how much more I could handle."

"Let's just keep praying that God gets ahold of their hearts," Herman said fervently.

That afternoon Linda glanced out the window. "Herman!" she called. "Look! The hooligans are in our yard!"

Herman walked out to where the boys were standing nonchalantly, smoking and lounging. "Oh, I thought you boys were gone."

José's face turned sullen, and his dark eyes smoldered. "What does it matter to you whether we are gone or whether we're here?"

"José, I'm not mad at you. I love you. But you all had said you were going to go away and work, so I thought I'd ask about it," Herman said calmly. He knew that the recent theft of some of the Yoders' personal property was probably weighing on the young man's conscience.

"Well, what does that matter to you?" José ground the dirt with his boot and spat the words out with vehemence.

"You matter to me, José. Your soul matters to me. And it matters to God too. All the things that have been happening recently are just indicators of something much deeper going on in your—"

"Stop talking to me!" José raised his voice in defiance. "Leave me alone!" He grabbed a knife from his pocket, snapped it open, and held it menacingly toward the bishop. "I'm going to stab you!" he snarled.

Without flinching Herman responded, "Well, I guess the sin will be yours and the glory will be mine. That's up to you if you want to stab me." His weathered face evinced both firmness and compassion.

This undaunted response angered the young man, who grew violent, sparring and thrusting his knife at Herman's midsection. But his empty threats failed to intimidate the bishop. Soon José slipped his knife back into his pocket, and without warning, he swung his fist and punched Herman under the jaw in an effort to knock him out.

For an instant the bishop felt as if he were floating away. He wobbled on his feet, but then steadied. His head cleared, and he looked at José, who now stood warily a few feet away from him.

"Son, this is not what you want to be. Think about what you are becoming. You are in desperate need of Christ. Your choices are not only costing you, they are costing everyone around you. Only the Lord can save us. I, too, was once a rebel, and the Lord saved me. I know He is waiting for you too."

Nonplussed by his neighbor's persistence, José slowly began to back away. Herman walked in step with him, calmly talking to him. When José reached his own door, the young man again pulled out his knife and made as if to stab him. "I am going to stab you, Herman! You better watch out!"

His eyes narrowed and his lips contorted into a snarl.

"Quiet down and stop doing that!" his mother snapped from inside the house. "Put it away."

With one last half-hearted but menacing thrust of his blade, José admitted defeat and put his knife away.

"Think about what I've said before it's too late, José. God bless you." Herman watched him go into the house and turned to go to his own home next door.

When José's older brother heard of the event, he was angry and humiliated. He came in person to extend an apology to Herman. "I am so sorry for the trouble José is giving you." Again Herman gladly extended forgiveness, but his shepherd heart ached for the day when José himself would express repentance.

In October one night at about 9:30, Kenneth's wife was getting ready for bed when someone started calling outside the door. "It sounds like José," she told Kenneth. "I wonder what he wants at this time of the night." Anxiety quickened her pulse. Kenneth answered the door, and Geraldina changed back into her clothes and went to see what was going on.

"José, you've been hurt!" She noted her cousin's scuffed-up face and bleeding arm and hands.

"Yeah, I was in a bit of an accident out on the pavement," José said.

Hurriedly Geraldina prepared some warm water with disinfectant and brought José a chair so he could sit down while she washed his wounds.

"What brought you here tonight, José?" Kenneth asked in his calm, deep voice.

José didn't look up as he spoke. "I guess I want to change," he said simply. "I don't want to keep on like this. I don't want to mess up my reputation any more than I already have, and I'm sorry for all the things I've been involved in recently."

Kenneth and his wife exchanged quick glances. José seemed to sense the questions that hung unspoken in the room. "I had an experience that made me think about things. I don't want to be known for stealing and vandalism and things like that anymore."

"Thanks for coming to us," Kenneth said softly. "We've been praying for you, José."

When Geraldina had finished washing and bandaging him, the young man stood to leave. "Thanks for helping me," he said quietly. As the door closed behind him, Geraldina looked at her husband in hopeful disbelief. "What do you think this means? Do you think he's repented?"

"He certainly seemed like a different boy tonight." Kenneth stroked his beard, deep in thought. "Time will tell if it's genuine. We'll keep praying. God is certainly at work."

Things quieted down after that. People began to breathe a bit easier. José even extended apologies to many of the people from church whom he had wronged. But he never showed up at church, and he didn't go to church elsewhere. The church prayed diligently for José, for Jorge and the others, and also for Marco, who was not living in the area anymore. As months slipped by, Geraldina sensed bitterness still lurking in her cousin José.

Some months later a neighbor warned them to tell Kenneth to be careful. "There is talk going around on Facebook about José wanting to take revenge on Kenneth for one time when he disciplined him as a child years ago."

The news startled and alarmed the Kropfs. One evening when Kenneth and Geraldina showed up late to a family mango peeling session, they reported that Marco and José had returned to the area and paid them a visit. "They were dripping with bitterness," Kenneth said, shaking his head sadly.

"And here we had hoped he wanted to change his life as he told us last fall." Geraldina's shoulders drooped.

"They said they wanted to come and talk to you about something important," Kenneth told Dennis soberly. "I don't know what they want, but it doesn't seem good."

It was Marco who contacted Rebecca. "When can we come and talk? Is Dennis going to be home today? I need everyone to be there." Dread filled Rebecca's heart at the prospect. What could Marco and José possibly want? And it struck a discordant note to hear Marco call her father by his first name. Before, he had always referred to him as Daddy, even after he left their home years ago.

Finally, late in the afternoon of June 9, 2014, it worked out for them to come and talk to the family. Rain was drizzling when they arrived. Rebecca invited them in for coffee and chocolate cake. It was Esther's last day at home before she left for a trip to the States, and Esther had made a nice supper and invited Kenneth's family, though Kenneth and his oldest son were gone. As Marco and José sat on the couch, they chatted and seemed pleasant enough, but they were messaging each other on their phones. "I guess we can't talk after all because Geraldina and the children are here," Marco finally said. They seemed loath to carry out their plan.

"Well, do you want us to go out on the porch or out to the bakery?" Rebecca asked.

"Yeah, that would be all right. But better the bakery. Better as far away as possible, because I don't think you are going to like what we are going to talk about," Marco said.

As they went from the house to the dim interior of the bakery, Rebecca felt heavy with dread. A drizzle still fell from the sullen sky above them and seemed to fit the mood that hung over the two young men.

Marco and José ushered the family in and then stationed themselves by the door. *Any way of escape is barred,* Esther noted apprehensively, glancing around the nervous circle.

Using his phone as a voice recorder, Marco announced, "Well, uh . . . we're here to talk about some things that happened long ago. Injustices, you could say." And while the family quietly listened, he began to pour out accusations. As he worked himself up and began to rave about "a damaged heart—proven by cardiogram" and "a twisted spine from clubbing" and "a lost childhood from too much work," they all realized that he had taken the normal childhood discipline of a loving, godly family and warped it in his mind.

He had brought José along as a witness. He accused Dennis and tried to get him to remember and admit to things so he could record his confession. He said that he had nothing against Judy and that he would defend Rosy because she always defended him, but he tore into Esther, after which he heavily accused both Rebecca and Dennis, saying that they had harmed him and ruined his life by holding him captive for four years.

"I went to a psychologist because everyone is always asking me why I am socially different, and I cried for four hours straight because of all the trauma and pain of recounting my life with you. When I was done, the man told me, 'You have to go see a lawyer, because these people have to be prosecuted.'

"And so I went to a lawyer. I can give you the psychologist's name and number, and I can give you the lawyer's name and number. The lawyer said, 'No, that can't go without punishment. You have to turn them in.'

"But, I'm not bad. I told him, 'No, I don't want to—I want to know what I can do to settle peaceably.'

"He said, 'Well, you need something tangible as restitution for all the injustice that you suffered.' "

Marco reached for his phone and showed them a portion of land that he claimed the lawyer had mapped out for him. It was the best part of their farm. "This is what I am asking for, and you have three days to make your decision. If you comply, everyone will be happy. And if not, I'll be happy and you won't."

Rebecca could sense the presence of the enemy in his threatening words.

But I feel the presence of God more strongly, she marveled inwardly. *His calming peace. Thank you that you are here with us, heavenly Father!* The threats continued as Marco declared that if they didn't give him the land, he would turn the church community in for abuse and get psychologists and social workers to investigate and interrogate all the youth in all the Mennonite communities for evidence of abuse. "A lot of people will end up in prison, and it will be the end of all the Mennonites in Costa Rica." His face glowered.

"I don't know if you have anything to say to defend yourselves," he challenged.

"I know we made mistakes," Dennis admitted freely. "And we are glad you came to talk to us about your trouble. If you are facing your pain and working through it, this means you can find healing. But what you are asking for is something we'll have to think and pray about. We can't give an answer right away."

"Well, I can't just say negative things." Marco's expression softened. "I did like it here. At first I thought it was the Garden of Eden. And you used to play with me on the floor, Dennis. I loved that so much."

"I hope you can forgive me for any mistakes I may have made," Esther said through tears. Rebecca had already apologized for several times when she had been more strict than necessary as a schoolteacher. But at the mention of forgiveness, Marco bristled. "No, we can't forgive. We have to have justice."

"Is this something that could be settled with money?" Rebecca asked cautiously.

"Oh, no. I know you need the money to care for the children. I just want the land. There is nothing else I'll take in exchange." Marco held unbending to his plan. José stood in the shadows, hard and silent, his form rigid with anger both young men held toward the Kropfs.

Toward the end of the conversation, Marco admitted, "You know, at first when we came here tonight, I saw the light in Rosy's little house, and I didn't want to come. You are taking care of all these needy children, and that's good. But José reminded me that we have to have justice. We need to get justice for the things that you did wrong. I was agitated to have to talk to you like this. You saw how hard it was for me. It felt so hard for me, and I just felt like clubbing you!" Anger, mingled with confusion and pain, contorted Marco's features.

"You can do as you like," Rebecca said quietly.

"No, we're with the law. It would go badly with us if we took things into our own hands," Marco said quickly.

"Besides, the punishment is heavier for harming women." José's voice was low and convincing. Rebecca shivered. José had thought through that already. What other vengeful schemes had he secretly entertained?

The young men seemed to take special note that Esther would be leaving for the States the following day and that she would return in July.

"I just want you to know we really care about you, Marco. We're sorry for your pain, and we pray that you can find healing. We truly do care what happens to you," Rebecca spoke for the family.

"Well, you have my phone number if you have any questions for me," Marco told them as the disturbing conversation drew to a close.

As the Kropf family stepped out into the darkness of a tropical night, their hearts were heavy with this strange turn of events. Who would ever have expected that taking a troubled little boy into their home would one day cause them to experience such blackmail and hatred?

The clouds hung low, and the rain had not let up. *Lord, what will the outcome be? How will this turn out?* Rebecca's heart cried as they walked slowly across the lawn to the porch.

Marco had left some of his belongings inside, but he hesitated at the door and asked. "May I come in, or . . . ?" He seemed to be testing their reactions to him now.

"Of course, come in!" Esther said. He followed the family inside, but José stayed in the shadows of the porch and waited, still sullen and silent. Rebecca fetched five jars of freshly canned mango sauce for her foster brother, knowing it was one of his favorite foods. He received it without much comment.

"It's raining outside. Let me take you home in the van," Dennis said.

"That would be fine." Marco seemed grateful for the offer.

With plans to leave the next day, Esther approached Marco to say goodbye. "God bless you, Marco." She gave him a sisterly hug.

Then he disappeared into the wet, dark night.

15

The Answer

With all that had transpired, it was hard to say goodbye to Esther the next morning. But both Rebecca and Rosy were glad she was getting a chance to go visit family and get away for a time. Esther had so anticipated this trip, and it was a gift from God that a family member from the States had loaned her the money to buy a ticket since she had spent so much of her savings on medical bills.

As they turned back to household tasks after she was gone, they felt emptiness inside. It just wasn't the same without their cheerful, industrious sister on the premises. But superseding this emptiness were the threats that loomed over them and the decision that lay before them. How would they answer Marco and José?

On Tuesday Dennis went into town with the other brethren to pass out tracts. Because the road noise inside the van was so loud, there was little opportunity for conversation and discussion, but he filled them in on the basics of what had transpired. At the end of the trip he asked, "Would you all agree that I tell him I've learned in life that when I make a hasty decision, it doesn't have a good outcome, and that I need more time to think about it?" All the brothers agreed this would be wise.

Wednesday was Marco's birthday. Rebecca remembered and made ice cream in preparation for his visit the following day.

When he arrived on Thursday afternoon to retrieve his answer, Dennis was ready for him. This time José had been unable to come, so Marco came alone. Taking out his recorder, he requested that Dennis speak in Spanish, "For my lawyer," he explained.

"Well, my answer is that I need more time to think before I can give you a decision," Dennis said.

Marco's face clouded. "Why didn't you tell me you needed more time?" His voice rose. "You made me come all the way down here just to say you don't have an answer ready?"

"We understood that you were okay if we need more time before we made our decision," Dennis said calmly.

"Yes, but you could have called me and told me you weren't ready yet." Marco seemed quite put out by this turn of events.

Just then Rebecca entered the conversation with an invitation. "Can you stay for supper, Marco? Yesterday was your birthday, so I thought we could celebrate together."

"No, but thanks just the same. It would be illegal for me to have dinner with you in light of what we are negotiating."

But when Rebecca brought out bowls of homemade ice cream, he did stay and eat it. They talked for a long time, and for a little while it seemed almost like old times. When darkness had fallen and he decided it was time to go, Dennis again offered to take him home, and Rebecca brought out more mango sauce. "As a birthday gift," she told him with a warm smile.

"Thanks," was his brief but seemingly heartfelt response. As Dennis drove him home, Marco turned toward him in the darkness and said, "I want to apologize for something I said about taking too long to answer me. You can have all the time you need to decide."

On Sunday during lunch, Marco called Rebecca and asked if they had an answer for him yet. It was June 15, 2014, the second anniversary of Judy's passing, and their cousins had come to visit. Rebecca handed the phone to her father, who took it with a look of resignation. "We have a meeting planned tonight to discuss this. I'll let you know what we decide."

Meanwhile, Esther was in the States enjoying time with family. She loved being with her brother and cousins, shopping at thrift stores and talking and laughing late into the night with girl cousins. But that Sunday anniversary of her mother's death was a painful day for her.

I have such mixed feelings, she thought. *Both anticipation and dread over tomorrow's reunion. With so many of Mama's relatives there, it will bring back so many memories.* She had grieved deeply and openly, but time did not remove the ache. As the extended family sat in a circle and shared memories of Judy, Esther jotted them down. Suddenly she couldn't take it anymore. Handing the notebook to someone else, she rushed out of the room, and finding one of her close girl cousins in the kitchen, she cried into her shoulder, letting her grief and pain flow out in a salty flood of tears.

When the tears had subsided, Esther said softly, "Something happened last month that brings me great comfort about Mama. It was when I was in the hospital with Andy for three weeks. He was deathly ill, and I didn't know if he would make it or not. He gets those horrible respiratory infections, and then he has to fight so hard to recover.

"It was the month before the anniversary of Mama's death, and Michael and Jessica had come to surprise us. The whole family was gathered, and we were going through Mama's things, but I was hardly able to be there with Andy being so sick. I felt so much sadness weighing on my heart through those days. Some nights I was getting hardly any sleep, which made it all the harder.

"One afternoon I was sitting in the hospital by a big steel door with black bars, having my quiet time. I was looking out over the town and away to the mountains, and I had my Bible open on my lap. The tears were flowing, and I was just asking God for comfort in all the sadness.

"And suddenly, when I looked up into the clouds above the mountains, it was as if a window appeared in the sky. It opened, and suddenly I saw Mama there, all radiant and happy, and she was waving to me. Just waving and waving, with that beautiful, heavenly smile on her face! Then she was gone. But I just felt so cared for, and I knew God was comforting me."

She smiled through her tears, and her cousin gave her a hug. "Thank you for sharing that with me. It must have been very precious to you. Just think, someday we'll join her up there, and we'll never face sadness again."

"I know. Sometimes I just about can't wait," Esther sighed. "But I know that it's important to live faithfully today so we'll be ready when that time comes."

· ·

Back in Costa Rica, the meeting about Marco's demand took place that night in the little church house in San Vito. The head bishop was present, and when it was decided that the church would fast and pray together for the next three days, he asked for a raise of hands of all those who would like to commit to fasting at some point during this united prayer vigil. It warmed Rebecca's heart beyond measure to see all the brothers and sisters raise their hands in promise and support.

Those three days of fasting and prayer drew them together, and when the brethren met on Wednesday night, they drew the unified conclusion that they would have to tell Marco and José no. They did not feel it would be right to give in to their threatening. "If they want to turn us in, then it's just going to have to be that way," the church body decided. They committed their lives, futures, and reputations into God's hands and parted ways.

Dennis's heart felt heavy as he faced the task ahead of him. He did not know how the young men would respond to his answer. On Friday morning he went to tell them, and Rebecca texted the church people, asking them to pray. "We are standing with you," several people texted back.

When Dennis arrived, Marco met him and said, "Let me go get José."

"That won't be necessary. I don't have anything to say except that my answer is no. I can't give you the land." Dennis spoke with quiet resolve.

"So your answer is no," Marco said flatly. His countenance darkened considerably, and when Dennis left a moment later, Marco sent a text hurtling into cyberspace to Rebecca.

"Here I thought you all had changed and were different now. But I see that's not true, and you are the same disgraceful people you always were."

Rebecca knew then that her father had given his answer. She wrote back, "God bless you, Marco."

His response came. "I assure you that you will lament this very much. By the end of this month, you are going to see your church close down. I am going to turn your family in. And after we do all this, it will be only the beginning . . ."

With trembling fingers she typed, "I love you, brother." For had not Jesus said to bless those who curse you?

Another text message dinged an instant later. "Don't be stupid. If you had any love for me, you would recognize that I deserve what I'm asking for."

"God bless you," was her only response.

He quit texting.

It wasn't long before the public health department came to pay a visit. Marco had turned them in for not having adequate bathrooms in their church building. The inspector, however, found no problems with the existing bathrooms. He only required that they add a handicapped-accessible bathroom, an emergency lighting system, and exit signs.

Soon construction for these requirements was underway. Not that these things were usually required of places in town, such as the bank. But because someone had reported them, the church was required to meet these higher standards. However, no one complained. They simply set to work while continuing to pray for their enemies.

Behind the scenes, more than one heart struggled to find peace in all that was taking place. How many more difficulties would they have to face before this ordeal ended? Yet above the unknowns, above the storm of threats and doubts and questions, was the overriding, solid faith in the goodness of God and His sovereign plans. He would not leave them, and He would lead them. Of this they were confident. And in this they sought rest.

16

Gone Missing

The quick, cheerful footsteps in the kitchen told Rosy that Esther was getting breakfast. *It's so good to have her back after her weeks in the States,* Rosy thought as she rolled over and sat up. Her head felt heavy. Just the day before, Rebecca had left for a conference in the States, and Rosy, who had moved into the main Kropf house to care for Rebecca's children while she was gone, had come down with the flu. Esther had brought her children up from her little house so Rosy could look after them while Esther went to clean. That morning, Esther had told Rosy to rest a bit longer than usual. Rosy could hear her sister singing snatches of song.

"What a fellowship, what a joy divine, leaning on the everlasting arms . . ." Like a songbird warbling its praise, Esther greeted the tropical dawn with her singing. Rosy dressed and went to help her with the morning's work.

After breakfast Esther read a psalm for devotions. Dennis was in San Isidro getting the van repaired, leaving only the two sisters and the little ones at home.

"You still don't look like you are feeling very well, Rosy." Esther brushed

Karla's long, dark hair as she helped the little girl get ready for school.

"My throat is sore, and I still feel really draggy and headachy this morning," Rosy said.

"I'll go get some leaves and make a poultice for you before Helen gets here," Esther said briskly. Helen, a British expatriate, had moved into their neighborhood several years before. Esther cleaned for her as a side job. Esther finished Karla's hair and hurried outside. Soon she had a warm poultice made and wrapped in a rag for Rosy's throat. "Hope that helps," she said kindly. "Don't worry about dinner. I'll make it when I get back from cleaning at Helen's. Try to rest if you can."

"Thanks." Rosy smiled gratefully. "I'll do what's needed with the children, and then maybe I'll sleep a little more."

"Helen is here to pick me up. Bye! I'll see you a little later." Esther picked up her bag, and then she and Karla were gone. Karla would be dropped off at school on their way out to the main road. Charlene had already walked out with Kenneth's boys a little earlier, but it was harder for Karla to walk that far. Rosy watched Helen's car go out the lane before dragging herself to the nursery to look after the children's needs. Soon she was finished and went to rest. The hours flitted by, and she drifted into a restless sleep.

Suddenly she jerked wide awake. Getting up and stepping out into the hall, she saw that the clock read ten minutes to one. *Esther should be here by now,* she thought with sharp concern. She tried texting her and calling her, but there was no answer. Then she remembered that Esther would have had to stop at school for their school-age girls, Karla and Char. *Maybe she's chatting with the teachers.*

I'm not that sick. At least I can start dinner so Esther doesn't have to do that when she gets back, she told herself. They still worried about the possibility of one of Esther's health issues causing her trouble when she was away from home alone. Messaging the teachers, Rosy soon received the message back: "Esther sent a message that she was on her way around 12:20 in the afternoon. She's not here yet. We sent Tim and Ezra to look for her. They went to the top of the hill but couldn't find her."

Knowing they needed to get the girls home and that she couldn't leave the children, Rosy texted the teachers to send the girls with Kenneth's boys. Rosy went to the bridge to meet them. When she got there, the boys commented that they didn't know what was wrong with Karla. "She made us run home from school," Ezra said breathlessly.

"We can't find Tato." Karla sounded near tears.

"Let's pray for her," Rosy said. She felt her own fears rising. "Lord, wherever Tato is right now, please be with her and keep her safe and bring her home soon."

The children weren't hungry. Char went to her swing where she always went when she was agitated or sad. She began to sing a song of her own making, and Rosy heard her singing the words, "I sure hope they find Tato, even if she *is* dead." Fighting tears and a mounting sense of worry, she dialed Helen, but couldn't get through. Then she called Sadie, a neighbor from the Kropf's church. "Sadie, we can't find Esther, and she won't answer her phone. I can't get through to Helen either. I'm worried." Rosy's breath caught in a sudden sob.

"We'll look for her," Julian's wife Sadie said. But she didn't sound worried. Rosy was afraid she was being a bit foolish, but she couldn't help how she felt. A bit later she called her father and asked him when he might be coming home. "Not till tomorrow. I have to wait for the van to get fixed," he said.

"You might want to come home sooner, Daddy. Esther is missing. They are out looking for her, but we can't seem to get through to her phone, and she isn't showing up."

Dennis sounded concerned. "I'll call Marlin right away," he said before he hung up. The anxiety mounted. Since their minister, Marlin, had been contacted, and Julian's family was going around the neighborhood asking if anyone had seen her, Rosy hoped they would soon have word. But when Julian's family suddenly stopped answering her phone calls as well, a sense of impending doom crept over her. She felt as if she must prepare for whatever was coming. With shaking fingers she combed back her hair and tried to compose herself.

Moments later Julian's van arrived in the lane. When she hurried out to see if Esther was with them, Rosy saw almost right away that she wasn't. *Something is terribly wrong,* she thought apprehensively as Sadie and her daughter Lois approached her silently. The two women each gave her a hug. But neither one spoke. Their haunted eyes told the horrible truth.

"What happened? Just tell me what happened." Tears welled up in Rosy's eyes.

Lois couldn't meet her eyes as she spoke the words in low tones. "She's not with us anymore. José killed her."

Shock gripped Rosy's heart. She would never remember it afterward, but a scream escaped from somewhere deep inside. Then she was sobbing. Karla and Char had come out on the porch, and Karla was wailing. Dazed, Rosy went to them.

"Did they find Tato?" Char asked.

"Tato is gone," Rosy said blankly. Suddenly she realized she hadn't asked Lois any questions about how they knew. She had simply believed her.

Coming back, she asked, "How did it happen? Did you see her?"

Lois shook her head. She had heard the news from her father Julian, who had gotten a call from Marlin, who had heard it from Herman. "I don't know. I didn't see her. The police didn't allow it."

"Well, they have to let me see her. She's my sister." Rosy's voice trembled.

"I'll stay with the children," Lois offered.

Sadie and Rosy climbed into the van, when suddenly she remembered they would need Esther's documents. Rosy rushed to get them, and when she got back to the van, Sadie's phone was ringing. As she climbed into the van, Sadie gave her the phone. "It's your father."

"Hello, Daddy?"

"Hello, did they find Esther yet? What is happening?"

"Daddy, Esther is with Mama." Rosy's voice was choked. Fresh pain shot through her each time she had to say it aloud. "José killed her."

Dennis was silent for a long moment. Then he said in a hushed voice, "I'll call Uncle Richard right away and ask him to bring me home. I'll be there in about two hours."

The drive was short, less than a kilometer, but not too short to tear the first *why* question from Rosy's anguished heart. "Why didn't God take care of her?" Julian didn't try to answer.

They rounded the last curve before they reached the scene. Police were everywhere, and people had started to gather. When they got out, Rosy approached an officer and asked to see Esther. "No, you can't," he said.

"She is my sister. I want to see her," Rosy said with calm firmness.

The officer's voice was husky as he replied, "It's better you remember her as she was."

Rosy's heart sank. "Why? Is she . . . beat up?" she faltered.

His answer was gentle. "Yes."

At that Rosy turned away. She had to tell people. She was the only family member there. As the texts and calls came in, she gave brief answers and bare facts. She had nothing else to give. Slowly her dazed, jumbled mind unraveled the sequence of events as it had happened. Esther had decided to walk home from Helen's place. José had ambushed her as she crossed the lonely ravine near their house. He had attacked her, pushing and dragging her down a long, steep embankment where he killed her. Her battered, bleeding body lay just five hundred meters from their home. A large stone lay crushing her head. Later Rosy found out that José had called Bishop Herman after he had committed the murder, and then turned himself in to the police.

Somewhere in those few terrible hours she got a call from Marco. He was sobbing on the other end of the line, "Can you forgive my family? I'm sorry for what José did. I'm sure he didn't mean to! Can you forgive us?"

Rosy assured him, albeit brokenly, that they would forgive them. Inside she felt shredded and frozen all at once.

As evening descended, she saw suddenly that José was sitting in the back of a police truck, right there on the scene. His face was turned away from her. He wore a red shirt that clung to him as if it were wet. Shocked at seeing him there, she asked a passing officer, "Can I talk to the young man?"

His face was unreadable as he turned to answer, "It's not advisable. He might turn violent and try to hurt you."

"Will you take him a message then?"

"What's the message?"

"We forgive you, and God bless you," Rosy said softly.

The officer's dark eyes were calculating as he studied her. Then his gaze went to the truck again. "Okay, you can come with me. I'll give you one minute." As they neared the truck, he added in an undertone, "Don't get too close, and only one minute."

José was lying down, handcuffed. The officer barked, "José, get up!" The young man hesitated, then slowly sat up, glancing up just enough to catch Rosy's eye briefly before dropping his head and averting his eyes.

"José, God bless you. We all forgive you, and we aren't going to seek vengeance."

That defiant but defeated figure would be forever etched in her memory. He did not look up as she spoke or when she had finished. With a lump in her throat, she turned to the officer. "I'm done. Thank you," she said quietly.

Dennis arrived a short time later. The only thought that went through Rosy's head as she saw his tall figure climb slowly out of Uncle Richard's van was, *How do you meet your father when his daughter has just been brutally murdered?*

She went to him. As he took her in his strong arms, she felt his shoulders heaving with sobs. For a few moments they cried together.

The *Organismo de Investigación Judicial* (Judicial Investigation Department) was there. The Red Cross had already left after pronouncing her dead and saying she had "injuries incompatible with life." Daylight faded. *I wonder why it's taking them so long to bring up her body out of the ravine,* Rosy thought. She shivered.

A neighbor lady hugged her, saying, "You are cold. Do you want a coat?"

"I'm fine," she responded dully. Finally they brought Esther's body, strapped onto a board, out of the ravine. By then darkness had nearly fallen. Rosy felt as if darkness were falling on her heart too.

When they reached over the back of the truck to touch the body bag containing the earthly remains of the woman they had loved so deeply, reality began to sink in. "May we see her?" Dennis asked in a trembling voice.

"Here, let us show you pictures," the investigators said. They clearly preferred this. The pictures held the digital date 7/23/14. Dennis saw the images of the crushed head and lacerated body on the investigator's camera. Evidently Esther had been stoned and beaten to death. Rosy stood off to the side, watching her father absorb the impact of those horrific photos. Something in her wanted to see her sister, but another part of her refused to look. Later would be soon enough to know the ugly truth.

Finally the officials left with the body, and the crowd scattered into the night. The family members who were there headed home. Someone had made supper, but no one was hungry. Karla played with her spoon and didn't eat. She hadn't eaten lunch either. Rosy sat down beside her and tried to help her eat. But Karla leaned into her lap with a heartbroken sob, and they sat there together, sharing tears.

That night Rosy had all of the invalid children to care for, so it was late before she dragged her exhausted body to the mat she had spread out between Karla and Char. She wondered when Rebecca would call. She pictured her oldest sister, arriving in a Texas airport from Central America, hearing the news of her sister's brutal death while far from her immediate family. Her heart hurt. It still didn't seem real. How could Esther be dead? But every time she drifted into sleep, she jerked awake to those same nightmarish words, "Esther is gone. José killed her."

17

Deep Calls to Deep

Rebecca stifled the scream rising from deep inside her. She didn't want airport security to come running. Uncle Bud stood quietly beside her. His last sentence still rang in her ears: "Esther passed away this afternoon." Rebecca had just landed in the States for the conference she was planning to attend. Never in her worst nightmares had she imagined she would receive such news.

The first disoriented thoughts that raced through her stunned consciousness were, *God, I prayed, "If something is going to happen, please don't let it happen while I'm gone." Why did it have to happen? My sister died, and I was not even there! I want this not to be true. You mean Esther has actually gone through that greatest experience which we all must face? It can't be. And Rosy—all alone with the children!*

Suddenly it hit her: *If she died, she had to die of something. How did it happen?*

"What happened?" she asked desperately.

Uncle Bud's eyes were brimming with tears, and his voice was full of compassion. "Someone killed her," he said softly.

Rebecca's hands flew to her face. She didn't move. She couldn't move. She couldn't swallow. Somewhere down a long dark tunnel was a tiny speck of light, and she felt far away. A ringing sound in her ears was all she could hear. *Was the murder connected with the young men who threatened us last month? Who did it, and how and where did it happen?* Questions tumbled through her mind like an avalanche, and an overwhelming sorrow threatened to bury her alive.

It felt so impossible. Doubt suddenly gripped her heart in a spasm of pain. Was it safe to trust a God who allowed such a thing to happen? She cried out inwardly, as a lost and frightened child cries out to her mother for reassurance. *Father, I need to know if she is in heaven with you. Is this really true? I need to know if it's true or not.* Her raw anguish and frightened anger burst out in her mind, *How could you let this happen, God? Where were you?*

Instantly God spoke to her heart, "At the same place I was when my Son was crucified." Rebecca found it strangely comforting to know God had lost His Son too. God understood.

Someone nearby whispered, "Do you think she's going into shock? Does she need water?" Rebecca shook her head, trying to clear her vision. She felt as if the real world was far away.

Uncle Bud and Aunt Betty took her home for the night. On the way home Uncle Bud explained what happened and answered the questions she asked.

When she walked into the spare room, her eyes immediately went to a motto on the wall. It read, "I am willing, Lord." Her raw heart wanted to scream, but instantly she knew—she wanted those words to be on her sister's memorial card. In the darkness of the night, her heart wrestled with wave upon wave of questions and grief. It was as if the psalmist's words were being wrung from her very soul, "Deep calleth unto deep . . . all thy waves and thy billows are gone over me."[1]

---

[1] Psalm 42:7

Her body simply would not stop trembling. Thankfully Aunt Betty had offered to sleep in her room that night; she lay on a mat on the floor sleeping. But even with her aunt close by, Rebecca felt alone. "God, I don't want to face another funeral. Please,"

Then, like a piercing bolt of lightning on a stormy night, the thought struck her, *Now we have to forgive them! And they said they could not forgive me.* Yet without hesitation she whispered, "In the name of Jesus, I choose to forgive them!" She made the resolve and refused to look back. "But the results, God—please, you have to get glory out of this if it's really true. You just have to." Her tears were still frozen in the shock of it all. Finally she drifted into merciful sleep.

The next morning she called home. Her father answered. "How are you?" he asked.

"Daddy, is it true? All that they are saying, is it true?" She spoke as one still clawing for hope.

His voice was husky. "Yes, it's absolutely true."

At this she burst into tears. Aunt Betty came to comfort her as she sobbed, her whole body heaving with the pent-up emotions. On the other end of the line, she could hear Dennis and Rosy both weeping softly. Finally she choked, "Can we view her?"

"Oh, no! In no way, shape, or form."

Her father's exclamation brought a fresh wave of sobs. Rebecca listened in horror as Dennis described how the murder had taken place. Her anguish was shortly submerged by a sudden wave of fear.

"Is it safe for us to be there? Will they come and kill us all?" Anxiety made Rebecca's voice tremble.

"God is in control, Rebecca. We have to trust Him. He is with us." Dennis's strong voice reassured her, but it didn't root out the fear that had sprung up inside her soul.

The long trip home was torture. The flights felt never-ending. But through the emotional fog and tears, she felt people's prayers holding her up. Michael, his wife Jessica, Kenneth, and his oldest son Victor were also flying from the States during those first two days, and all of them would later say the same.

At 3:00, in the darkness of early morning, Dennis and Rebecca pulled into the lane. Rosy and Charlene were waiting for Rebecca on the porch. They fell into each other's arms and held on for dear life. "I guess now it's just you and me," Rebecca finally choked out. Rosy didn't answer, but her extra-hard squeeze spoke volumes.

Dennis joined them in the living room, and they talked till 4:30. Rebecca found out then that José had turned himself in to the police. "We don't know if it was remorse or if he simply knew he was going to be caught sometime and he would get a lighter sentence if he turned himself in. We wonder, though, if he had plans to harm Herman as well. When he first got to Herman's house, he asked Herman to follow him to a deserted place and talk. Herman refused, and that's when José told him he had killed someone. I doubt we would have found the body if he hadn't shown them where it was. It was so far down the ravine and away from the road." Dennis spoke steadily, but the traumatic experience had clearly aged him.

As they talked, Rebecca found out more than she wanted to imagine about what had befallen her sensitive sister and the gruesome way her life had been taken. How could someone be so barbaric? They concluded that demonic hatred had influenced the young man. Their only comfort in the face of such horror was that Esther was safely in heaven now.

Finally their exhausted bodies collapsed in sleep. When Rebecca got up several hours later, the subtle nuance of death lingered in the house. The pitcher and water glasses on the table, the bouquet of flowers with a note attached, suitcases sitting by the wall that belonged to the friends just arriving, Esther's little ones sleeping in the spare bedroom. Lucille, the bishop's daughter, moved quietly around the kitchen preparing breakfast for the family and their guests, and caring for the children. But the strongest reality of all was an echoing absence. There was no brisk, cheerful appearance of Esther herself.

When Myrtle Bates came from the bedroom that morning where she had been sleeping, Rebecca gave her a long hug. "You were one of the first people I thought of when I heard the news. I am so sorry," Rebecca breathed. Esther's bosom friend must be feeling the pain as much as they were.

In a hushed tone Myrtle responded, "Don't feel bad for me, Rebecca. I feel terribly bad for you!"

Two days after Esther's death, on Friday around dinnertime, they received the call that the autopsy was completed and the body was on its way to the morgue at the hospital. The funeral wouldn't be until Monday, July 28, 2014.

When the family met the truck at the morgue, they didn't open the body bag, but they touched Esther's hands through the white plastic barrier. Not until after Esther had been buried did her family think about honoring her memory by clothing her body for burial. The mortician had simply wrapped her body in a quilt and placed it in a body bag before it was released to the family.

They inquired about a casket. They wouldn't purchase it till the following day, but plans had to be made. *How does one plan a funeral like this?* Rebecca wondered wearily. None of their brains wanted to function in an orderly manner.

One of Rebecca's hardest tasks since Esther's passing had been to tell Esther's two little ones about it. Even though Kimberly and Andy couldn't really respond, she knew they missed their Mommy. "Mommy's in heaven now," she had whispered gently to them. And they seemed to know it somewhere deep in their precious little souls—Mommy wasn't coming back. For several months afterward, Kimberly sank into a deep depression and didn't smile or laugh. Andy almost instantly got deathly ill.

When he started with fever that continued to rise that Saturday, they took him to the emergency room, where he was admitted. Rosy stayed with him that first night. In the following days, he sunk so low they wondered if he would make it. It seemed to be his body's way of coping with his sudden loss.

That night when Rosy woke from a weary sleep at about 3:00 in the morning, she saw Rebecca in a room down the hall from her. Startled, she went to inquire. Gerald had been in need of some medical attention, so Rebecca had brought him in to the hospital. "We three girls are all here together," Rebecca said sadly. Esther's body lay in the hospital morgue.

By 6:00 Sunday morning Rebecca had to go back home, and Rosy stayed only a few hours longer. Gerald's birth mother came to be with him. Rosy felt awful leaving Andy. But Esther's friend Anabel, who had lost a special-needs son, was coming to be with him a bit later, and Rosy would be back that night.

After the viewing that night, Rosy got back to the hospital at 10:00. She desperately needed sleep, but a nurse came by and wanted to talk. Several staff from the hospital had just been involved in an auto accident, and a nurse who was well known to the Kropfs had been killed.

Later one of the church girls would tell how the van had plunged off the road and down the cliff behind their house, and how they had gone to the scene to help. As she was helping the dying nurse, she spoke to her of salvation and helped her pray. It was a comfort to the Kropfs to think that both their sister and the nurse who had been a subject of her prayers had passed into glory so closely together.

The next morning when the men came to get Esther's body, Rosy turned Andy's care over to Anabel and went to join the rest of the family. Today was the funeral. How they dreaded the final goodbye!

On the blackboard behind the pulpit, the words were written boldly: "My Father, where were you when this happened? Answer: The same place I was when MY SON was crucified."

Both funeral messages were filled with the power of forgiveness, the shortness of time, and the need to be ready to meet Christ. *Every time there is a funeral, there is one less family member to comfort each other,* Rebecca thought drearily. It all seemed dull and heavy and hard. Every one of them was sleep-deprived and worn out with grief. Yet somehow a strength greater than their own fortified them to testify the goodness of God in the face of such loss.

At the graveside the sun beat down mercilessly. People carried umbrellas to ward off its scorching rays. To Michael it was the saddest funeral he had ever attended. Not only would he never hear his older sister's voice again this side of glory, but the stark reality of the result of a life abandoned to sin stared him in the face. His heart hurt for those young men who had heard the Gospel and hardened their hearts to this point of evil. *Lord, rescue their souls before it's too late,* he prayed inwardly. *Bring them to repentance.*

As the last clods of dark earth were shoveled over that fresh grave next to Judy's and the last notes of the last hymn died away, something in Rebecca ached to just cry and cry. Rosy, too, felt nearly crushed with grief. But Esther was buried now, and Rosy's feelings seemed to be submerged too deep for tears. The words echoed still over those verdant mountains, "My Father, where were you when this happened?"

And in the midst of all the anguish and pain and turmoil came the bracing reply, "The same place I was when *my Son* was crucified." The One who had once known the anguish of the cross to bring eternal redemption interceded that they might have the strength to say, "Not our will, but yours, be done." And in the reflection of His heart and character, their hearts were strengthened to echo, "Father, forgive them; they do not know what they do. Into your hands we commend our lives. Father, glorify your name."

18

Desired Haven

ear ran rampant through the mountains in the following days, especially among the women and girls. It seemed that the murder was
not the end of the story. Newspapers were coming out with false
reports. Slander was being spread about the Mennonite community, and
threats of lawsuits and prison were poisoning the air, already laced with
the tension of such brutal grief. It seemed as if all hell had encamped
against God's people.

"I am just so afraid," Tonya, a local believer, told Julia, the minister's wife.
Tears quivered in her dark eyes. Rebecca and Rosy stood in the little circle
of women conversing after church. Tonya had put words to their own inner
struggle. Tonya, whose husband had left her years before, lived with her
four children at the bottom of a lonely gully. She went on. "I don't even
want the doors open during the day. My brother told me I can't live in fear;
I have to overcome. But I feel as if I'm in a deep hole of fear no matter how
much I pray." Tonya wiped her tears and looked pleadingly into Julia's face.

Julia slipped an arm around Tonya as she replied, "When Mark Yoder's family was here recently, they shared a song with us that has blessed me so much. It's the hymn 'How Firm a Foundation,' and it has suddenly taken on a whole new depth after these recent events. A couple of the verses especially stand out to me:

> Fear not, I am with thee, O be not dismayed;
> For I am thy God, and will still give thee aid;
> I'll strengthen thee, help thee, and cause thee to stand,
> Upheld by my righteous, omnipotent hand.

> When through the deep waters I call thee to go,
> The rivers of sorrow shall not overflow;
> For I will be with thee, thy troubles to bless,
> And sanctify to thee thy deepest distress.

> The soul that on Jesus has leaned for repose,
> I will not, I will not desert to his foes;
> That soul, though all hell should endeavor to shake,
> I'll never, no never, no never forsake! [1]

"These are promises we can hold onto, Tonya. No matter how dark it gets."

Rebecca turned away from the little group, her heart in turmoil. She longed to find that place of peace and refuge in God, but she didn't know how to handle the brutal attacks of fear that had plagued her since Esther's death. She had learned in the days soon after the funeral that it was very possible that she had been the one José originally planned to kill. Now fear haunted her. She was afraid to step close to the windows for fear someone would shoot from the edge of the woods. She was afraid to leave the back porch to feed the chickens in case of a sudden ambush.

And though she insisted to herself that God was in control, she could

---

[1] "K" in John Rippon's *Selection of Hymns,* 1787.

not convince her trembling, shattered emotions that God's hand was the safest place to be. Pictures of Esther's horrific murder screamed at her that this was not true, even though she continued to choose to believe the truth of God's omnipotence. Every night she quoted Scripture desperately to ease her heart and mind enough to fall into a troubled sleep. For her, the world had lost its beauty. The days passed on leaden feet.

Finally she could no longer handle it. *I'm desperate. Something has to change,* Rebecca decided. It was Sunday afternoon. The house was stiflingly hot, but not as stifling as the inner heat of the turmoil and fear. She knelt by her bed and cried out, "God, I can't go on like this! Please deliver me somehow, because I can't! I can't keep functioning if I have to carry all this fear."

Gently His Spirit prompted her with the thought, *Ask God to take the fear away. That would be deliverance.*

"Lord, please take this crushing fear away," she prayed simply. "I want to trust you. Thank you that you are still good even in the midst of all of this."

"It's a miracle," she whispered the next morning when she awoke. She had slept soundly through the night. As she cared for the children that morning, she suddenly remembered that last evening when the dogs had been barking, it had caused her no fear, unlike the panic their barking had aroused for so many days in a row before that. She now walked erectly again. And for the first time in weeks, she could see and let her soul be nourished by the inviting beauty of the tropical world outside her window. Even the warmth of sunshine suddenly mattered. The fear was gone!

"Lord, you are so good!" Tears of gratitude welled up in her eyes. "I'm free again. Thank you so much."

The family had started a thanksgiving journal soon after Esther's funeral, a way to focus on the good things God had done and was continuing to do. Under a heading of "We Are Thankful," different family members recorded the gifts God had given them in the midst of their pain. Now, in her gently lilting script, Rebecca added, *"That God answered my prayer and removed my fear. Oh, praise His name! Glory be to God in the highest!"*

Previous entries testified other family members' thankfulness:

1. That *"If God be for us, who can be against us?"* [2]

2. That Esther never had to see the pictures that came out in the newspapers.

3. That God knows the truth of all the matter.

4. That the law is concerned for our safety.

5. For the support of the brethren in many places.

6. That though Esther was robbed of her dignity of being properly dressed for burial, no one could rob her of her robes of white.

7. That God is carrying our grief and understands our questions.

8. That the girlies remind us again and again in song, *"How beautiful heaven must be . . ."*

Often they heard either Char's dynamic voice or Karla's happy one warbling the refrain of the song:

> How beautiful heaven must be,
> Sweet home of the happy and free;
> Fair haven of rest for the weary,
> How beautiful heaven must be. [3]

For it wasn't only the adults who had to process their grief and fears; the little girls had their share of processing. Nine-year-old Charlene attempted to journal how she felt. More than once she wrote in large, expressive letters:

José killed Tato. He had no right to kill her. But we must forgive José. We love him.

---

[2] Romans 8:31

[3] Mrs. A. S. Bridgewater, ca. 1920.

For Karla, healing came in the form of something Rebecca had prayed for soon after Esther passed away. Rebecca had asked God for some confirmation that Esther was safely in heaven with Him.

Sometime later when Karla told her mommy, "I saw Tato in heaven," Rebecca thought at first it was something her little girl was simply making up. But when Karla insisted, she stopped to listen. Karla told her that she had seen Esther, wearing white, at the gates of heaven, and that she had waved at her and told her she was very happy; that she had seen several evil men on earth who wanted to harm her family, but that God and Jesus were watching them from heaven; that Jesus had told her that when it was her turn to die, Jesus would take her in His arms. Whether it was a dream, or how God had given these vivid pictures to her, they would never know. But to Rebecca it was another gentle reminder that God was with them in each step of this story, even in the smallest details, teaching them to pour out their pain to Him in trusting worship.

During this time of persecution and turmoil, one of the ministers shared a message from Mark 4 with the little congregation tucked away in the mountains. Rebecca took notes as she listened, knowing she would want to ponder these passages more. The minister told how the storm had come up while Jesus was asleep in the boat. Jesus wasn't somewhere else. He was very present with them. But it wasn't until they cried out to Him that He chose to respond. He was in control the entire time. But when He spoke, the storm was stilled and a great calm ensued.

This fit well with another set of verses the minister read from Psalm 107. The psalm describes suffering one affliction after another, including the vivid depiction of a storm at sea with waves churning violently out of control. Then it goes on to say—as Rebecca paraphrased from her Spanish Bible—that "when they cried out to God in their anguish, He brought them out of their affliction. He changed the storm to a whisper, and the waves were still. Given that calm, they were glad, and God brought them to their desired haven."

As Rebecca took notes, she realized that these verses, in Spanish, didn't say that God calmed the storm, but rather that He changed it out, replacing it with something completely different. He did not merely stop a force, but took something that was wild and totally out of control and changed its nature entirely. God could do that in the midst of what they were facing! He could change José's heart. And He could give each one of them the change of heart they needed to respond to the afflictions He was allowing. He was not merely a God who could stop the storm. He was a God who could change its nature as well!

The minister went on to ask, "What is God's purpose in the midst of the injustices of life? Ephesians says He chose us for 'the praise of His glory.'[4] And John says that 'herein is my Father glorified, that ye bear much fruit.'[5] In the face of the tempests we are facing, God's desire is that we respond with love and joy and trust in Him that brings peace. Even when He chooses not to still the external tempest, He has the power to bring calm to the internal one so we can face the trials with joy and confidence, knowing He is in control. It is in Christ that we find our eternal haven both now and in eternity. In this way we fulfill His purpose for us and bring Him glory, no matter what the devil tries to bring against us."

And someday we'll reach that desired haven, thought Rosy wistfully. *How beautiful heaven must be.* She had camped in Psalms in all the weeks since Esther's passing, and ever so slowly her shattered heart was beginning to mend as she fed on the words of truth and took shelter in His promises. Sometimes the circumstances screamed that there was no earthly haven. But she knew that God was her Refuge and Strength. She believed it even when she could not feel it at all.

Beside her, Rebecca was thinking the same thing—that even in the

---

[4] Ephesians 1:12

[5] John 15:8

midst of their journey to that final haven, God promised to bring calm to the tempest in the soul. He had proven this. Even on the days when the sisters wanted to scream to fill the painful silence, God had unique and beautiful ways of ministering His peace and grace to walk through their sorrow. Most meaningful of all was His presence and the way He filled the silence with His comfort.

He did not always choose to remove the pain. But His presence was always with them. Had He not promised, "My presence shall go with thee, and I will give thee rest"?[6] And as He had proven by taking away Rebecca's fear, she was confident that when the time was right, He could also bring them out of their present afflictions.

The refrain of the closing hymn floated out over the mountainside as the little congregation sang their faith to their King, even in the face of tribulation, their voices blending in stirring harmony.

> I've anchored my soul in the Haven of Rest,
> I'll sail the wide seas no more;
> The tempest may sweep over wild, stormy, deep,
> In Jesus I'm safe evermore.[7]

---

[6] Exodus 33:14

[7] Henry L. Gilmour, 1890.

Epilogue

The tropical sun hung hazily in a cerulean sky, warming the verdant valleys and rocky plateaus of the Costa Rican countryside. Tonya and her children hurried up the dusty road toward the bus stop. Mountain peaks tumbled above them, their blue rock reaching to embrace heaven. Clouds were beginning to gather on the horizon. Tonya hoped it wouldn't rain while they were in town doing their shopping.

As they mounted the steps of the great rumbling bus, Tonya's children suddenly hung back. They had spotted José's mother Lola on the bus, and after all that had taken place, they were prone to fear. Pushing her children gently ahead of her into their seats, Tonya stopped.

She had known this woman a long time through her pain and choices and hardships. She also knew how Lola, who was no longer attending church, had seemed so hard-hearted in response to Esther's murder and never apologized for what her son had done. But suddenly in spite of all she knew, Tonya felt a great compassion surging up within her for all that this mother's heart must have suffered over the past months. Reaching out her arms, she gave her a quick hug and kissed her cheek in the traditional warm greeting.

José's mother was hesitant, but something almost like hope flickered in her dark eyes. She smiled a little and then turned back to her window. Tonya went to her seat with a heart that sang. Slowly, with the passing of months, her fear had begun to dissipate too.

For the Kropfs, life continued with the normal rhythms of caring for the children and wading through the ups and downs of the grief journey. Bit by bit they were beginning to see glimmers of glory in God's workings as well.

Someone Rebecca barely knew had told her that when they heard that the family had chosen to forgive José, they had been challenged to forgive in their own set of painful circumstances. Others shared how the Kropfs' strong faith and unwillingness to leave because of the threats was impacting their own desire to embrace whatever hard things the Lord allowed in their lives. These testimonies aided the slow process of healing for the family, glimmers of light in the dark days to bolster their faith in God's unknowable purposes.

A month before José's trial was to be held, Dennis and a friend happened to drive past José's mother as she walked along the road. On impulse he turned around and came back, offering her and her daughter a ride. To his surprise, she accepted.

On the short drive to her destination, she apologized for the way she had spoken with Dennis right after the tragedy. "I freely forgive you." Dennis spoke with fervency, his heart welling with gratitude that she was exhibiting more friendliness and less of the painful bitterness of a year ago. As she prepared to exit the vehicle, Dennis's friend turned and spoke, "We know this time must be very difficult for you. We are praying for you."

A year after Esther's passing into glory, the official court trial was held. Dennis and Rosy, among others, were called upon to testify. It was a long week while they waited for the verdict. Would José be released? They did not know. But they felt the grace of God carrying them through every hour in court and every waiting hour at home. They knew the matter was in God's hands.

In the final hours before the verdict, both Dennis and José were given an opportunity to speak to the judge. "God has put you in place to judge such things. I leave it all in God's hands. I will support whatever you decide," Dennis said simply.

"I leave it in God's and your hands, letting you do justice," José's response was quiet and resigned.

The judges determined that they were going to commit José to a mental institution for treatment and for the safety of society for the time being. When all was said and done and everyone was dismissed, Rosy could hardly believe it was really finished. It had seemed to drag on for so long. Now suddenly, just like that, it was over.

In an update to praying friends and family, she wrote:

God was so wonderful through it all, and we marvel at so many details He took care of so easily. We are so grateful for the support and prayers of so many, many people. Thank you to each one for remembering us and praying for us. Please keep praying, for us and José and his family. We long to reach them and feel like there is so little we can do.

So they wait and pray for the day God brings these precious souls to Himself. And as Rebecca put it, "My mind goes into the future, and I hope someday José will come back as Joseph's brothers did years later, in repentance. I want to tell him those same words: 'You meant it for evil but God turned it into good.' For Esther it was only gain, as we put on her memorial card: 'For me . . . to die is gain.' "[1]

But for the family and the community, the grief and the trauma of the death of someone they loved so deeply is far from over. Fear, questions,

---

[1] Philippians 1:21

waves of soul-deep pain, and all the varied emotions that come with grief—including, anger, remorse, and emptiness—are part of the journey in different ways for each heart. The fact that they must daily see the place where the event took place is slowly losing its sharp edge of anguish, but the pain remains as a part of their story. They will never be the same. They can only trust the unknown to God and allow Him to hold their hearts and bring the redemption that sometimes only He can see. And as they look to Him for healing, even in the moments of deepest pain, a doxology flows heavenward.

Acknowledgments

Aboard the plane on the way to Costa Rica to begin this project, I felt God whispering to my heart that He had unique plans for this book project. "This is about hearts more than about a story," He seemed to say. And in every part of the writing of this book, this has proven true. I have learned in new ways the depths of desire and passionate love with which God pursues and heals our hearts as He brings us into fuller and more yielded communion with Him. Above all, He wants our hearts!

As always, a special thanks goes to my personal editing team: Patti L., Barb S., and Lizzy L. Each one of you has gone beyond proofing pages and cared for my heart so well through so many miles. Thank you especially for walking so closely with me in prayer and insight through the joy and anguish of scripting these pages.

Thank you to G.J. Hoffman for all the shared hours of writing. I love having another author as my best friend!

Thank you to Dennis Kropf for sharing honestly and humbly. But even more for walking humbly with your God in the midst of great loss.

Thank you to Rebecca Kropf for hours of labor and help in research, for candid sharing, for your sensitivity to God's heart and leading, your uproarious sense of humor, for loving so well, and for letting me into your heart so quickly and wholeheartedly. You have taught me so much in the short time I've known you, and you have become an invaluable friend.

Thank you to Rosy Kropf for showing me what it means to live forgiveness in the face of the darkest evil. For your loyalty and your gentle strength, for letting me into your life in such deep ways and for always asking how I really am. You are close to my heart!

Thank you to Esther Kropf, who lived a life full of passion for Jesus and laid down her life for her King. Your example has challenged and inspired me in incredible ways. You are deeply missed and not forgotten.

Thank you to the Kropfs' church community, who willingly and graciously shared of their lives and experiences through interviews and hospitality. Thank you for being examples of Christ-like love to each other as you walked with the Kropfs and lived the pain and victory with them, especially in the year following Esther's death.

Thank you to all of Esther's friends who shared so willingly of their time, letters, and memories. Your help was instrumental in bringing a fuller picture of Esther's heart and life and the hearts she shared it with.

Above all, thanks to my Redeemer, Jesus. My purpose for writing comes from you. May these pages bring hearts closer to yours, for your glory.

About
the Author

Rachael originates from the lovely Northwoods of Minnesota, but currently lives in the Middle East. Some of the things she enjoys in this season of life include international travel, sunsets and sunrises over the ocean, drinking coffee and tea with friends from diverse backgrounds, building meaningful friendships in another culture, and seeing the night sky's star constellations from another side of the globe.

She continues to embrace the opportunity of writing as God opens new doors. "To be a scribe recording just one small chapter of His story as He works among His children is a privilege," she says. "When I write, I feel His pleasure, and it's my heart's desire that what flows from my pen would be for His glory alone."

Rachael enjoys hearing from her readers and invites you to email her at ascribebytrade@gmail.com. You may also write to her in care of Christian Aid Ministries, P.O. Box 360, Berlin, Ohio 44610.

About Christian Aid Ministries

Christian Aid Ministries was founded in 1981 as a nonprofit, tax-exempt 501(c)(3) organization. Its primary purpose is to provide a trustworthy and efficient channel for Amish, Mennonite, and other conservative Anabaptist groups and individuals to minister to physical and spiritual needs around the world. This is in response to the command to ". . . do good unto all men, especially unto them who are of the household of faith" (Galatians 6:10).

Each year, CAM supporters provide 15-20 million pounds of food, clothing, medicines, seeds, Bibles, Bible story books, and other Christian literature for needy people. Most of the aid goes to orphans and Christian families. Supporters' funds also help to clean up and rebuild for natural disaster victims, put up Gospel billboards in the U.S., support several church-planting efforts, operate two medical clinics, and provide resources for needy families to make their own living. CAM's main purposes for providing aid are to help and encourage God's people and bring the Gospel to a lost and dying world.

CAM has staff, warehouses, and distribution networks in Romania, Moldova, Ukraine, Haiti, Nicaragua, Liberia, Israel, and Kenya. Aside from management, supervisory personnel, and bookkeeping operations, volunteers do most of the work at CAM locations. Each year, volunteers at our warehouses, field bases, Disaster Response Services projects, and other locations donate over 200,000 hours of work.

CAM's ultimate purpose is to glorify God and help enlarge His kingdom. ". . . whatsoever ye do, do all to the glory of God" (1 Corinthians 10:31).

The Way to God and Peace

We live in a world contaminated by sin. Sin is anything that goes against God's holy standards. When we do not follow the guidelines that God our Creator gave us, we are guilty of sin. Sin separates us from God, the source of life.

Since the time when the first man and woman, Adam and Eve, sinned in the Garden of Eden, sin has been universal. The Bible says that we all have "sinned and come short of the glory of God" (Romans 3:23). It also says that the natural consequence for that sin is eternal death, or punishment in an eternal hell: "Then when lust hath conceived, it bringeth forth sin: and sin, when it is finished, bringeth forth death" (James 1:15).

But we do not have to suffer eternal death in hell. God provided a sacrifice for our sins through the gift of His only Son, Jesus Christ. "For God so loved the world that he gave his only begotten Son, that whosoever believeth in him should not perish, but have everlasting life" (John 3:16).

A sacrifice is something given to benefit someone else. It costs the giver greatly. Jesus was God's sacrifice. Jesus' death takes away the penalty of sin for all those who accept this sacrifice and truly repent of their sins. To repent of sins means to be truly sorry for and turn away from the things we have done that have violated God's standards (Acts 2:38; 3:19).

Jesus died, but He did not remain dead. After three days, God's Spirit miraculously raised Him to life again. God's Spirit does something similar in us. When we receive Jesus as our sacrifice and repent of our sins, our hearts are changed. We become spiritually alive! We develop new desires and attitudes (2 Corinthians 5:17). We begin to make choices that please God (1 John 3:9). If we do fail and commit sins, we can ask God for forgiveness. "If we confess our sins, he is faithful and just to forgive us our sins, and to cleanse us from all unrighteousness" (1 John 1:9).

Once our hearts have been changed, we want to continue growing spiritually. We will be happy to let Jesus be the Master of our lives and will want to become more like Him. To do this, we must meditate on God's Word and commune with God in prayer. We will testify to others of this change by being baptized and sharing the good news of God's victory over sin and death. Fellowship with a faithful group of believers will strengthen our walk with God (1 John 1:7).